100 Tips for Reducing Your Anxiety

Worry Less, Sleep Better, and Enjoy Life More

Gareth Loken

Contents

Part I: The Basics

If your anxieties keep you awake at night, you're not alone. Surveys have shown that roughly one third of the population suffers moderate to severe anxiety at some point in their lives. That's a lot of anxiety that does nobody any good.

100 Tips for Decreasing Your Anxiety is here to help. In this first section, you'll find 70 simple suggestions to help you recognize, manage, and decrease your daily worries.

1. It's OK: You Suffer from Anxiety

Your family and friends probably describe you as *nervous* or *high-strung*.

"Oh, he's a worrier," they say. "He's been like that as long as I can remember."

"She always thinks the worst is right around the corner," they say. "She's been like that since she was a little girl."

Your co-workers say you're tense, on edge, keyed up, overwrought, worked up, jumpy, twitchy, jittery. You know they're right, but you can't help it—it's just the way you are, you insist.

Like millions of other people, you suffer from anxiety. Your built-in flight-or-fight response is perpetually activated, which means you can't relax because your body is preparing to defend itself from some perceived threat.

You take your worries to bed with you, tossing and turning because your mind won't shut down. The only energy you have is the nervous energy that goes with your never-ending attempts to stave off tragedy.

And there's always a dark shadow lurking in the corners: worries about your job, concern for your kids, the fear that you'll run out of money, the likelihood that you'll sit in hellish traffic on your morning commute. Like your anxieties, the list is endless.

By saying "Anxiety is a problem for me," you take the first step in controlling it. This book offers 100 simple suggestions to help you get through the days and sleep through the night. Some of the suggestions are easy to implement; others take more work and commitment. Choose the tips that work for you, and share them with the other anxious people in your life.

2. Talk About It

Anxiety is nothing to be ashamed of. With the amount of stress that humans encounter daily—family responsibilities, company downsizings, continued offshoring of work, corporate greed, broken political systems, enormous income inequalities—it's not surprising that you're anxious.

Now that you've admitted your anxiety, it's time to talk about it with the people in your life. Sometimes your closest friends and family members ratchet up your anxiety without being aware of it. If they can make small changes to help lessen your anxiety, ask them to do so. Maybe your teenagers stay out late without telling you where they are or what time they're coming home. Explain the effects on your anxiety level and ask them to help you to become a less anxious person by sending a text or making a phone call. If you and your spouse have different approaches to the spending and saving of money, discuss not only the dollars and cents but also the connection between money worries and your anxiety. (For more information on coping with money worries, see Tip #71.)

Be careful, though. Don't make the conversation all about you. If you're asking for a favor, give something in return. If the kids promise to text you when they're going to be late, you can promise in return not to nag them about cleaning their rooms. If your spouse agrees to spend less, you can return the favor by planning romantic but inexpensive outings, such as a picnic or a walk in the park.

With help from the people in your life, you'll be well on your way to reducing your anxiety to a more manageable level.

3. Take Charge

Even if you suffer from generalized anxiety—constant worry about almost everything—you can likely list specific situations that make your heart feel as if it's going to beat out of your chest. Maybe the thought of getting on airplane sends you scrambling for the nearest liquor bottle. Or you're required to attend a company sales meeting or other business event, and just thinking about it leads to large, unsightly patches of wetness in your underarms. Or you're invited to a get-together, but you hate parties, and you know that the moment you can find an excuse to escape, you will.

Rather than allowing these specific anxieties to rule you, own them and take charge of them. Refer to the following tips for some simple ways to take back your life from the most common anxiety triggers.

- Money: Tip #71
- Children: Tip #72
- Air travel: Tip #73
- Parties and other social events: Tip #74
- Family get-togethers: Tip #75
- Your health: Tip #76
- Your job: Tip #77
- The dating scene: Tip #78
- The holidays: Tip #79
- Public speaking: Tip #80

Avoidance isn't a good long-term solution. Instead of trying to creep around these triggers, you need to go through them or climb over them. View them as jobs that must be done, assignments that must be completed for you to get an A in life.

12

4. Turn Off the News

The journalist's motto is "If it bleeds, it leads." In other words: The more violent and bloody the event, the more you'll see of it.

As an anxious person, do you really need to see nonstop coverage of murders, rapes, mass shootings, child molestations, natural disasters, war, genocide, and every other atrocity that humanity has to offer? No, you do not.

Self-described "news junkies" obsessively follow their chosen news channel, usually the outlet that matches their political beliefs. So, in addition to reading about, hearing about, or watching the worst things that happen on Earth, they also get to be spectators at nasty political battles as the commentators inflate local, domestic, and world events with incendiary political rhetoric.

"But," you may say, "I need to be an informed person. I can't just bury my head in the sand and pretend that the world doesn't exist. I can't be an airhead who exists in my own private bubble."

Fair enough. Read your local community newspaper (it needs your support) and subscribe to a weekly news magazine. *The Week* will do a great job of keeping you informed while offering multiple perspectives on the same story.

5. Don't Follow the Weather

Hurricane! Tornado! Earthquake! Landslide! Tsunami! Nor'easter! Torrential rains! Flash floods! Storm surges! Blizzards! Wildfires! Gale-force winds!

No matter which type of meteorological Armageddon is predicted, you can be pretty sure that most of the time it won't add up to much: a few downed utility lines, some inconvenient power outages, road closures here and there.

But in the hours before the big storm, you'll get to watch your neighbors preparing for the Apocalypse. The shelves of the local grocery store will be empty as people prepare to hunker down for untold weeks. Not a bag of ice melt or sand can be found, anywhere within a hundred-mile radius. The toilet paper and Clorox wipes have disappeared from the supermarket shelves, never again to be found at reasonable prices. You go to bed convinced that, during the night, your house will be lifted from its foundation, and you'll wake up in the Land of Oz.

Aren't you fed up with the panic mongering that meteorologists spew from your television set? Haven't you read one too many hysterical weather-oriented websites whose homepages scream with headlines of weather-related disasters somewhere in the world, even if that weather event is taking place on the other side of the globe?

Do a specific act of kindness for yourself and stop obsessively tuning in for updates, and repeat this mantra: "I have no control over nature. The best I can do is be as prepared as I can be." (See Tip #6.)

This isn't to suggest that you should ignore truly important, dangerous, or destructive weather events. But you should get your information from sources that seek to protect you rather than make your blood pressure skyrocket. Sign up for text alerts from the National Weather Service or local reports that keep residents informed. When those sources say you should take certain steps, then take them.

In the meantime, turn off the network news and save yourself the heart palpitations.

6. Be Prepared

What happens if the power goes out for a week? How will I survive if a snowstorm traps me in the house for ten days? The company's downsizing; am I next on the chopping block?

Nobody knows your anxiety triggers better than you do. Now, instead of worrying about something that may or may not happen, get ahead of the curve. Prepare for the worst. By taking action, you transform the worst-case scenario into a "not great, but I can deal with it" scenario. Now there's no longer a black beast lurking in the forest just beyond your doorstep. Now there are just some pesky deer who keep eating the plants that cost you a hundred bucks at Home Depot.

Worried about starving to death in a snowstorm? Buy plenty of canned goods (and a manual can opener) and store them in a cool, dry place. Have flashlights and plenty of batteries on hand. Fill up your bathtub with water in case you need it. You know all of this already—now do it.

Terrified that a lump is a tumor? Get yourself to the doctor and find out for sure. Knowledge is power, and Western medicine has many effective treatments.

Do you see the writing on the wall: Layoffs are happening, and you're on the chopping block? Start networking like crazy, polishing up your résumé, and taking industry colleagues to lunch. Assume that you won't find an equal-paying job right away, and that you may end up taking a pay cut. Prepare your plan for cutting your expenses and living frugally.

And so on …

7. Use Your Commute

As commuting times increase on all modes of transportation—car, bus, subway, ferry, airplane—mature, well-adjusted grown-ups have taken to breaking down in tears. The aggressive driving—the congestion—the rubber-necking that turns a 10-minute drive into an hour-long ordeal—the accidents that could have been avoided if the person behind the wheel had been driving rather than texting—At some point it all becomes too much, and what's an adult to do but sit and sob in frustration?

The mere thought of their daily commute is enough to make anxious people start quivering. They don't know what the day's commute will bring, but they know it will be something horrible.

So turn that horrible, anxiety-provoking experience into something quasi-pleasurable. Listen to books on tape or podcasts, saving your favorites for your commute. Learn a new language. Subscribe to satellite radio so that you can listen to your favorite type of music or a comedy station so that you can laugh even though you haven't moved for half an hour. If you're alone, sing at the top of your lungs.

Work from home as often as you can, or try to negotiate hours so that you're not commuting at peak times. If you drive, download an app that gives you real-time traffic reports that detour you around the worst pile-ups and nastiest tangles. By de-fanging your commute, you de-stress your life. And when you de-stress your life, some of your anxiety goes dribbling down the drain. Good riddance to it.

8. Quit All Social Media. Now.

Instagram. Pinterest. TikTok. Even worse, Twitter. Worst of all, Facebook. Does social media make you happy, or does it make you miserable?

If it makes you happy, you're a member of a small and lucky minority. Every serious research study into the topic has shown that the more time that people spend on social media, the more unhappy, depressed, and lonely they are. It's hard not be depressed when everyone is implying or stating outright that they're better informed than you are, they're better looking, they have more fabulous lives, and they eat more beautiful food at fancier restaurants. If you follow anyone or anything on Twitter, you run the risk of being humiliated, canceled, or emotionally obliterated if you say something controversial in your 288 characters.

Does your anxious self truly need to receive an endless feed of angry political messages, incomprehensible likes and dislikes, and inflammatory and possibly faked news? Do you need to get drawn into the personal dramas of people you don't really know and probably don't even like? Do you enjoy (a) having someone else's religion shoved down your throat, or (b) having your religious faith disrespected?

You dislike, or hate, all these things. So why do you tune in? It's time to drop out. Taking part in social media is like walking a tightrope between two skyscrapers during a windstorm. It's not a matter of whether you will fall. It's when.

Delete your accounts now. Use the time that you otherwise would have wasted on social media in doing some good. Volunteer. Visit an elderly family member. Meet a flesh-and-blood friend for coffee. Do something that will make you feel good about yourself and appreciate what you have instead of buying into other people's fantasies about themselves and their lives.

The saddest, and most joyous, part is: Nobody will notice that you've gone.

9. Enjoy a Warm, Relaxing Bath

Bath (noun): The process of immersing oneself in a tub filled with water.

Optional equipment: a book, rubber duckies, bubbles.

The idea of a bath seems so quaint and old-fashioned today, so out of step with the modern world. Saying that you're going to luxuriate in a warm bath gives the impression that you're not busy, you're not important, you have time to waste. Successful, professional, in-demand people barely have enough time for a shower, much less a bath.

Ironic, isn't it? Just a century ago, a bath was a luxury reserved for royalty and nobility. (Think *Downton Abbey*—did we ever see Mrs. Patmore or Mr. Carson luxuriating in a bathtub?) Today most homes have at least one bathtub, and most of the time it's used as a surface on which to stand during a shower.

Research has shown that people who are deprived of touch and human companionship benefit from taking baths; the feeling of being surrounded by liquid warmth is extremely comforting and relaxing. One study even showed that one-hour bath can burn as may calories as a half-hour walk.

If you can't remember the last time you took a bath, find twenty minutes this week to do so. Make the water as hot as you like, and add a cup of Epsom salt as the water run. Then just lie back and relax … no cell phone, no television, no interruptions. As you lie there focusing on the sheer pleasure of it all, your worries will go into remission, at least for a while.

Aim for at least one bath a week, but that's a minimum. Want to enjoy a bath every night until you get past the latest round of stressors? Do so, and love every minute of it.

10. Break the Rumination Cycle

You're sitting in traffic, going nowhere fast, and your mind starts to wander. Suddenly a thought intrudes: Your boyfriend/girlfriend did something yesterday that annoyed you. The more you think about it, the more your annoyance turns to frustration, and then anger, and then out-and-out rage. By the time you get home, you're spoiling for a fight. Rather than forcing your mind to think more pleasant thoughts, you kept your worries alive by thinking about them in detail, over and over.

Psychologists call what you've done *rumination*, which is also linked to depression. When not occupied with other tasks, the human mind tends to dwell on, and exacerbate, the negative. Take a moment to think about your own experiences with rumination. When was the last time you thought nonstop about all the good things in your life? Your answer is probably "Never."

Rumination is terrible for anxiety. It takes all your worries and blows them out of proportion. Small problems balloon into massive obstacles. Fleeting emotions morph into relationship-ending dramatics. Reasonable thoughts about all that you need to accomplish become gut-wrenching, detail-oriented examinations of the challenges you face and the inevitability of failure.

The solution is simple: Stop ruminating. When you find yourself getting into a negative thought loop, force yourself out of it. Listen to some upbeat music or find another method of distracting and entertaining yourself. There's no shame in watching a ridiculous sitcom that makes you laugh. Try *Bewitched*, *I Love Lucy*, *Everybody Loves Raymond*, and other shows that usually don't push a political or social agenda that you may not agree with. There's nothing wrong with binge watching if you're feeling particularly cranky or anxiety-filled.

One key to breaking the rumination cycle is to recognize it when it begins. When you find yourself thinking obsessively about possible negative outcomes of unpredictable events, force your mind away from its worries and toward something positive. Put in your ear buds and listen to music, or think about something you're looking forward to, such as a weekend with friends or attending your child's school play. Actively examine how the rumination is making you feel (anxious, lousy) and make the decision to your dismantle your negative thought cycle.

11. Master Your Gadgets

Sociologists sometimes speak of the "digital divide"—the gap between those who have steady access to technology and those who don't. Often the discussion is couched in terms of socioeconomic status: The wealthy have technology, and the poor don't.

We can also think of the digital divide in other terms. Of those who have access to technology and use it daily, many simply do not understand how that technology works or—worse—what to do when something goes wrong. For example, you likely have a complicated set-up of cable box, TV, DVD player, and remote control with a minimum of 100 buttons. Push the wrong button and your TV stops broadcasting the channels you want to watch. Do you know how to get your TV back on track? Can you use the basic applications on your mobile phone without becoming hopelessly lost? Do you know that you can solve most computer issues by closing out of your programs, shutting down your computer, unplugging it, and then rebooting?

The underlying fear that your technology controls you—rather than the other way around—is terrible for anxiety. So take action. Write down all your questions about how to use your cell phone, your TV, your remote control, your wireless doohickies—and then hire someone to teach you how to use them and how to fix common problems. You likely have a family member who'll do it free—probably the same person you've been driving crazy by calling for technical support.

Write down all the answers and procedures, and practice them so that you know what to do the next time the television won't turn on.

Extra credit 1: Write down all your usernames and passwords in one place, and keep the list updated as you change passwords (as you will be forced to do occasionally).

Extra credit 2: If you fear that pushing the wrong button on your computer will cause it to blow up, invested in an automatic cloud-based backup service. Then you'll never have to worry about losing your files or your work.

12. Tune Out of Politics

There's a good chance you have pretty strong political beliefs. Right or left, conservative or liberal, centrist or progressive, Red or Blue, coastal or center-of-the-country, Northeast or South, California or Texas: You know what you think, and nobody's going to convince you otherwise. Yes, occasionally (VERY occasionally) there will be debates and Q&A sessions between level-headed people exploring the pros and cons of a given issue, but you'll have to search hard to find such respectful back-and-forth. But: Even after you've listened to the most eloquent pro-Choice or pro-Life advocate speak, will you change your views on abortion? After you've watched two people duke it out over Second Amendment rights versus the number of gun deaths in the United States each year, will your opinion about gun control have changed?

No. With rare exceptions, your opinions will remain the same as they have always been. You may think, therefore, that it makes sense for you to listen to, watch, or otherwise tune into media that support your beliefs. Why, then, does watching your favorite news channel make you frantic with anxiety? The answer is simple: What lies beneath the reporting of the "news" is the desire to whip you up into a frenzy, to solidify your loathing for the other side, and to addict you to a never-ending cycle of anger, even rage.

What can you do? Stop giving the media control over your emotions. Tune out. Turn off CNN or Fox. Stop reading *The New York Times* or *The Wall Street Journal*. Instead of listening to far-right or far-left radio talk-show hosts, download podcasts that teach you about history, philosophy, literature, or any non-political topic that interests you.

"But," you may be thinking, "Why should I jettison my deeply held beliefs?" The answer is: You should not, but work within a realistic range of possibilities. Donate to the causes you believe in. Write to your congressional representatives. Support the candidates whose values match your own. Most of all, vote.

The next time your blood starts to boil as you watch a newscast, remember: He who angers you, controls you. Take back control and enjoy the benefits as your anxiety diminishes.

13. Get Out—Or Move Out—of the City

According to the United Nations, more than half the world's population lives in cities. If you live in a city in North America, you share your urban life style with 82% of the North American population.

Much has been written about the benefits of urbanization: the environmental sustainability, the walkability, the reasonable commute, the culture, the arts, the public transportation. And there's no denying that cities offer all these benefits, and many more.

But there's a dark side to city life, too. They're expensive. Crowded. Noisy. Stressful. Numerous studies have shown much higher levels of neurosis in cities, along with the higher stress levels that come with literally living on top of one another. Your anxiety isn't being helped when you can't get into a packed subway car or bus during the morning or evening commute, and you likely don't feel relaxed and happy when your upstairs neighbor is clomping around in work boots while you're trying to sleep. It's impossible to walk on clouds of tranquility when you are sharing the streets with (literally) millions of other people.

Just getting out of the city for a weekend can be a balm for the soul, a tranquilizer for the anxious. Hop on a train or a bus, or rent a car, and go somewhere with low population density and plenty of trees. Watch videos, read, sleep in, and breathe in the air. If you find your heartbeat accelerating and your anxiety level of rising on your return trip to the city, it may be time to consider moving out for good. The idea might not be as untenable as it seems, now that so many companies offer remote work options.

14. Stop Liking Your Anxiety

- Do you (secretly) like your anxiety?

- Does your anxiety allow you to justify your behavior?

- Do you use your anxiety to manipulate people and situations?

You like your anxiety when:

Your worries give you the excuse you need to drive your coworkers crazy with your micro-management and obsessions.

You argue that being a good parent means (and requires) constant vigilance regarding every aspect of your children's lives, to ensure they make all the right decisions, as defined by you.

You offer your "nerves" as the reason why you haven't fulfilled your obligations as an adult.

Your family walks on eggshells around you for fear of making your anxiety worse, and the scenes that sometimes go with that.

If you're serious about finding the calmer, less anxious you—then stop liking, and milking, your anxiety.

15. Detach Yourself from Technology

Nothing will keep your anxiety in high gear like holding onto your phone for dear life, craving that text message, that comment, that email, that photo, that Tweet from a social influencer, that meme starring the cat or dog du jour. With your phone in your hand, or next to you at your desk or dinner table, or (yes) while you're using toilet or having sex, you keep yourself in a state of constant anticipation. Your body remains keyed up, and you mind remains on high alert.

Many of us remember life before cell phones, tablets, and laptops. We got through our days. We did our jobs, spent time with our families, read a newspaper (remember them?), made time for our hobbies, called friends, made plans to get together. Our lives were no worse for not being attached to the Matrix 24/7. We were less instantaneously informed, but the news came to us eventually. Most importantly, we didn't have a pocket computer to keep ourselves ready to panic at a moment's notice.

We can bring those days back, and calm ourselves, by turning off our technology. Before you turn in for the night, put the phone and any other device with a glowing screen in a separate room. Meals should always be technology-free, with no exceptions. The same goes for gatherings of any type. Be present in the moment instead of trying to capture it.

In other words: Decrease the amount of input into your life. By doing so, you'll decrease the unwanted output (anxiety and the many other negative effects of technology addiction too numerous to list here).

16. Give Up Your FOMO

Fear of missing out, or FOMO, is based on the concern that other people are having experiences that you aren't. The result can be a sort of social panic that the world is leaving you behind while others have a dizzying array of experiences that make your life seem dull, dull, dull and pathetic, pathetic, pathetic. Not surprisingly, social media feeds FOMO. How good can you feel about yourself, really, when you're taking a nap in a pair of old sweats while the members of your social network post photos of the fabulous meals that have just been placed on their tables at trendy restaurants, or send around photos of the gorgeous sunset on Maui, where they've rented a cottage for two weeks?

FOMO keeps you perpetually on edge. There's so much to do, and you want to do all of it. As a result, you overload your schedule, running hither and thither. You don't enjoy the moment because you're thinking that you could be having *more* fun and making *more* contacts and meeting *more* potential lovers if you'd done something else instead. You're on steady high alert, always looking for that next opportunity to be included or to take part.

Recognizing your FOMO is the first step to doing something about it. Make a list of your priorities. What is most important to you? What activities do you find most enjoyable? Conduct a cost/benefit analysis: What are the pros and cons of accepting or not accepting an invitation? When you begin to assess each social opportunity in terms of what it promises versus what it delivers, you may find yourself thinking, "No, I really don't want to go have drinks with those colleagues, as I don't like them very much" or

"So what if everyone's waiting in line to see that exhibit of the Abstract Expressionists? I like Italian Renaissance art much better."

When you accept that you can't see, do, or experience everything that the world offers, you take charge of your emotional well-being and lessen the anxiety that FOMO creates.

17. Challenge Irrational Beliefs

The pioneering psychologist Albert Ellis identified twelve irrational beliefs that can increase anxiety and depression. The key to improved mental health, he believed, is actively challenging each belief to reveal its inaccuracy. These beliefs are:

- To feel loved, I must have sincere love and approval almost all the time from all the significant people in my life.

- I must prove myself to be thoroughly competent, adequate, and achieving in all respects.

- People who harm me or commit misdeeds are wicked or evil, and I should blame, damn, and punish them for their sins.

- It is terrible when things are not the way I want them to be.

- Emotional troubles are caused external events, and I have little ability to control my feelings or rid myself of anxiety and depression.

- If something seems dangerous or worrisome, I should obsess and worry about it endlessly.

- It is easier for me to avoid life's difficulties than to face them.

- Anything that strongly influenced my life once continues to determine my emotions and actions today.

- It is awful when I do not quickly find good solutions to my problems.

- I can achieve happiness by doing nothing.

- I must have perfect control over things.

- My general worth and self-acceptance depend on the quality of my performance and the degree to which people approve of me.

Do you ever fall into these thought traps? If so, examine each belief as it enters your mind. Consider Ellis's first irrational belief: "To feel loved, I must have sincere love and approval almost all the time from all the significant people in my life." Even though you occasionally fight with your spouse or children, and even though they may not agree with all of your decisions, does it make sense to believe that they stop loving you because you've argued about whether you should go out for Chinese food or Italian food?

By breaking down and eliminating each irrational belief, you can greatly diminish the anxieties that keep you feeling unhappy, nervous, ill at ease, and jumpy.

18. Gently Manage Your Anxious Friends

There's probably someone in your life who tries to manage his anxiety by increasing yours. Whether in person, on the phone, in text, or in email, he doesn't seem satisfied until he's worked you up into a state of near-panic.

Maybe he's worried about the big virus that's going around—Don't you agree that the entire human race is now one step away from death? Perhaps she fears an upcoming recession—Aren't you worried that you're going lose every penny of your retirement savings and spend the rest of your life dumpster diving? Or he's obsessed with being ripped off—Aren't you tired of being robbed by your dentist, your doctor, your mechanic, your landscaper, your accountant, your lawyer? By the end of the conversation, you're ready for a tranquilizer, because no matter how often you try to change the subject, Friend or Family Member circles back to the worst-case scenario, that black sucking vortex from which there is no escape.

It's time for some relationship management. Take a step back. Don't answer or read texts. Let the call go to voice mail. If your worrier works with you, find yourself slammed with work and unable to go out for lunch or drinks. Make a reasonable excuse: You've been overworked, or you're coming down with (or getting over) a cold, or you have a previous commitment.

When you must get together or risk losing the relationship, try to spend time with your nervous friend in a group setting. Your person will likely discover rather quickly that she's the least popular person at the party and will sing a different song, at least for a while. In short: If you're nervous, avoid nervous people.

19. Exercise

Exercise of any kind—whether a leisurely stroll, a jog, a ride on a stationary bike, or hardcore fitness training—has many benefits, including improved health, better sleep, and improved self-esteem when you see results. It's also a terrific way to cope with anxiety.

The problem with anxiety is the way it takes over your mind and won't let you focus on anything else. As a result, you get trapped in a never-ending loop of worry, worry, and more worry.

When you're on a treadmill, you need to pay full attention to your legs and breathing. When you're lifting weights, you've got to focus on maintaining your form and keeping the weight balanced. Even when you're walking through the neighborhood, your attention is likely to be grabbed and held by things you've never noticed before: a plant, a tree, an architectural detail, a neighbor's questionable taste in window dressings. When your mind is engaged with other things, the worry can't get through.

If you make exercise a part of your daily regimen, you'll soon find that you don't want to do without it. Even if you're a reluctant exerciser, you'll be won over by the physical and mental benefits. Start slowly if you have to, and consult a physician before you do anything hardcore. If there's a time of day that worry overtakes you—that's the time to exercise. (The exception is nighttime before bed. You don't want to stimulate your body shortly before it needs to fall asleep.)

20. Avoid Social Comparison

Ever since Robin Leach began shoving the lifestyles of the rich and famous down our throats (thank you, Robin), we've become envious of the now-much-more-visible 1 percent.

Social comparison has long been with us, though. The phrase "keeping up with the Joneses" comes from a comic strip that began publication in 1913. Cartoonist Arthur Momand had a great deal of fun drawing the exploits of the social-climbing McGinis family, who were forever trying to keep up with their neighbors, the wealthier and better-placed Joneses. *Keeping Up Appearances*, which ran on the BBC from 1990 to 1995, showcased middle-class Englishwoman Hyacinth Bucket (which she pronounced "Bouquet") in her never-ending quest for social betterment.

Many of us are now on a quest to drive the newest car, find the most exotic hotspots (with photos to be posted on Facebook), eat at the fanciest restaurants (with photos to be posted on Instagram), buy the most expensive jewelry (to show off at cocktail parties), and to have the biggest houses with the most elaborate landscaping (in which to host cocktail parties for those we wish to impress).

If the previous paragraph strikes a chord of familiarity in you, then you're likely increasing your anxiety by your concern over what others think of you. It's a losing battle; no matter how many strides forward you take, the goalpost moves further down the field. So stop chasing the goalpost.

21. Try Meditation or Yoga

Disconnecting your mind from its worries is essential to managing your anxiety. Just as you can exercise your body, you can train your mind to prevent it from becoming a runaway train.

Meditation works at clearing your mind and, in the process, relaxing your body, allowing both to achieve a greater calm. Meditation need not take large chunks of time. Some people find that they can relax themselves by meditating for just a few minutes a day.

Busy, harried, and anxious people can easily find excuses to dismiss mediation. "Won't work." "Not for me." "I'm not into that New Age stuff." But at least *try* it. There are hundreds of websites and apps devoted to the many different types of meditation practices and techniques. Surf around until you find one that appeals to you. Then try it for at least a week, going into it with an open mind—one that may find some relief from its fears, doubts, and concerns. Some apps you might check out are Buddhify, Calm, GPS for the Soul, Headspace, Insight Timer, MindFi, Omvana, Sattva, Smiling Mind, and 10% Happier.

If you are a more active person, you might try yoga instead. Yoga combines breath control, body postures, and meditation to help you achieve a state of inner calm. Like meditation, there are many different types of yoga. Do some research and look for the type that fits best into your interests and abilities. An added benefit of taking a yoga class is the possibility of forming new friendships, which often brings continued motivation to keep attending classes.

22. Create a Sanctuary

Virginia Woolf wrote of the need for a room of one's own. Specifically, she meant that a woman must have "money and a room of her own if she is to write fiction." But the idea has come to mean more generally that everyone needs private, quiet space in which to take a nap, pursue a hobby, escape the world, or do anything else that nurtures the soul free from the prying eyes of the world.

People with anxiety are often stuck in the everyday worries of their world—and, sometimes, in the doom-and-gloom stories that come to us from every corner of the globe. Creating a sanctuary allows you to put a metaphorical (and sometimes a physical) door between you and the world. In your sanctuary, you say, "Nothing comes into this space that upsets or bothers me. This is a place of fun, peace, relaxation, anything that takes me away from the negative outcomes I worry about and that prevent me from living the life I want to live."

If you own a home, it may be easy enough to create a Man Cave or Woman Cave in an unused room, basement, or attic. But you needn't live in a house to have a sanctuary. You might set off a small part of one room with a screen, or a curtain. Once you've done that, enforce Sanctuary Rules: No visitors. No Internet. No politics. Regardless of where you locate your sanctuary, make it comfortable and fill it with things that give you pleasure just by looking at them.

You can also create a sanctuary outside your home in a public space. You might choose a corner at your local library, a couch at a Barnes & Noble, a quiet table in a coffee house. After you've made a place your own, you may find that just thinking about that place helps you relax.

In the 1970s sci-fi thriller *Logan's Run*, Logan 5 says, "There is no sanctuary." But there is, and you get to choose where to put it.

23. Find Your Flow

The psychologist Mihaly Csikszentmihalyi (pronounced "Chick-sent-me-high-ee") recognized that humans are happiest when they are in a state of flow: completely absorbed by a task that they find challenging but not frustratingly difficult. When you're in your flow state, time slips away. You look up from whatever you're doing and realize that hours have passed.

While you've been in your flow state, your anxiety has receded into a distant corner of your mind, maybe even disappeared completely. As you're writing your novel, practicing your musical instrument, building models, or doing anything that interests and challenges you, you're using your skills and feeling a sense of accomplishment when you finish a task or make a breakthrough.

Csikszentmihalyi also identified other emotional states that are created by the combination of skill level and challenge level, as follows:

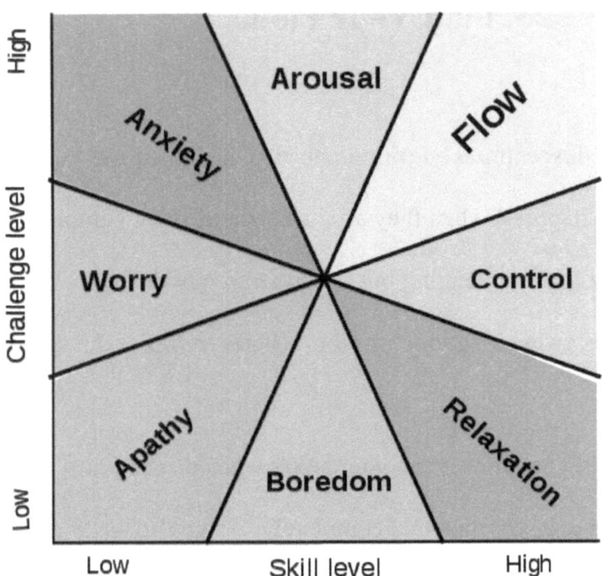

Note where anxiety and worry occur: When the challenge level is too high, and your skill level is too low. So, as you embark on new hobbies or challenges, start slowly. You're not going to be a concert pianist after two months of lessons. You won't become the next Michelangelo with your first set of paintings. Take the time to learn and to find your flow, and progress to the next level when you feel ready to do so.

Also notice that relaxation—the opposite of anxiety—occurs where skill is high and challenge is low. So, when you're feeling anxious, do something you're really good at, something that doesn't challenge you. You'll feel pleased with your expertise and keep some of your anxiety at bay.

24. Unclench Your Fist

Anxiety does terrible things to the body. You know the effects: migraines and other types of headaches, exhaustion because you haven't slept well, unpleasant gastrointestinal effects that we need not get into …

Becoming aware of two common bodily manifestations of your anxiety will work wonders.

First, monitor your fists. Are they clenched for no apparent reason? Take a moment to check them while you're lying on the couch or in bed. As soon as you realize they're clenched, unclench them. You'll feel an almost instantaneous sense of relief and release. The mere act of loosening your fingers and allowing them to rest in their normal, relaxed state will liberate some of your anxiety. Next, remain aware of what your hands are doing. When they start to ball themselves into fists, remind yourself to relax them. In essence, you'll be telling yourself: I control my body. My anxiety doesn't.

Second, check your jaw. Does it feel like a vise that's attempting to snap your head off your neck? Follow the same advice above: When you notice your jaw getting tight, relax it. A good long yawn can help, and there's nothing wrong with a bit of jaw exercise to move it around. If you grind your teeth at night—because your partner has said that you do, and it's probably driving him or her crazy—it's time to see the dentist. Teeth grinding can have terrible long-term effects, and dentists offer some miraculous and relatively inexpensive treatments.

25. Don't Hold Your Breath

Do you ever find yourself holding your breath for no apparent reason? You may be lying in bed—and holding your breath. Or sitting at your desk—and holding your breath. Or reading a book—and holding your breath, and not because of the suspense.

One of the best ways to monitor and deal with your anxiety is to be aware of your breathing. Short, shallow breaths don't help with anxiety, but long, deep breaths do.

Give it a try right now. Take a long deep breath that fills up your lungs and brings much-need oxygen into your body. Now try it five or six more times. Many people who try this exercise find that their body actually tingles from the pleasure of the oxygen rush.

There's another benefit, too. While you've been focusing on your breathing, you haven't been thinking your boss, your kids, your spouse, the mortgage, the neighbors' barking dog, the mounting bills …

If you've ever had a panic or anxiety attack, you've probably learned that the best way to deal with it is to breathe slowly and deeply, sometimes into a paper bag. It's not that the paper bag does anything magical; it's that focusing on deep breathing helps you bring your mind under control.

So, the next time you find yourself holding your breath, let it out. Then reward yourself by taking a few deep breaths. Try taking a few deep inhales when you turn in for the night, too. It's a great way to tell your body that it's OK to fall asleep.

26. Cut (Way) Back on the Caffeine

What's the most consumed drug in the world? Aspirin? Acetaminophen (Tylenol)? Ibuprofen? Marijuana? Opioids?

No—the most consumed drug in the world is caffeine, not surprising when you think about how much coffee, tea (hot and iced), and colas we consume in a typical day. Much like sugar, caffeine gives us an energy boost to start our day or to perk ourselves up before a big meeting. You can even buy tablets and energy drinks that boast enormous amounts of caffeine to keep you flying high.

Because caffeine is a stimulant, it won't come as a surprise that it keeps your body on high alert and unable to relax. If you're already anxious, heightening your body's state of readiness will only make matters worse.

You may think you don't ingest an unreasonable amount of caffeine, but caffeine can be sneaky. You'll find it in some unexpected places, such as chocolate, certain sodas, coffee and chocolate flavored ice creams, and even headache medications.

So: Watch your caffeine intake throughout the day. Instead of refilling your coffee cup, fill up your water bottle. If you're not a water drinker—and a lot of people aren't—then look for caffeine-free labels at the supermarket. Many tasty iced teas and colas have no caffeine, and you likely won't miss it. If you need an energy boost during the day, try a protein snack rather than mainlining caffeine.

If you have difficulty sleeping, stop your caffeine intake after 3 P.M. If you're an early-to-bed/early-to-rise person, just say no to caffeine after 12 noon. You'll fall asleep faster and sleep better.

27. Laugh

Nothing will send your anxiety packing like a good belly laugh. It's tough to dwell on your worries when you're busy laughing.

With the Internet and TV/movies on demand 24/7, there's no reason for you not to have a steady supply of humor. Don't feel guilty about watching older, gentler sitcoms; sometimes, the more preposterous they are, the better. The purpose of the laugh track is to get you laughing, and it works. Laughter is contagious, and it's one of the antidotes to anxiety.

You can even buy a Bag of Laughs, or some other laughing device, from one of the novelty companies. It's simple enough: Insert the battery, push a button, and you hear a person laughing his (or her) head off. Try buying one—you can get them for under 10 bucks. You may be amazed by how quickly your laughing starts to accompany the recorded merriment.

A word of caution: Avoid the mean-spirited nastiness that tries to pass for comedy. (Certain stand-up comedians: You know who you are.) That type of comedy taps into anger, resentment, frustrations, and many other anxiety triggers. You may find yourself simultaneously laughing and becoming angry at the "truth" being spoken. Don't let anger anywhere near your laughter.

28. Try an Herbal Supplement

Many natural, herbal, and homeopathic treatments are reputed to help with anxiety. As with most supplements, there is very little scientific proof that allows us to say "This will absolutely, without a doubt help you manage your anxiety," but many people swear by them. There's also the placebo effect to consider: If you think it helps with your anxiety, then it does.

All of the following are available singly or in combination. You will likely need to experiment to see which work for you.

- 5-HTP
- Ashwagandha
- CBD oil
- GABA
- Holy basil
- L-theanine
- Lavender
- Lemon balm
- Melatonin
- Passionflower
- St. John's Wort
- Tryptophan
- Valerian root

Some people swear by Restoril, which is marketed and sold over the counter as an anxiety reducer. Others sing the praises of Hyland's Nerve Tonic and Rest formulas, also available over the counter.

If you do decide to experiment, check with your doctor first. Monitor your reactions closely, and if you experience any unusual symptoms, stop taking the supplement immediately and schedule a follow-up visit with your doctor.

Also keep in mind that many of these remedies are gentle or take time to take effect. They aren't tranquilizers that hit you like a ton of bricks, but they may lull you gently into a less anxious state or even sleep. Again, monitor your reactions until you find what's right for you. Equally important, don't use supplements as your sole way of dealing with anxiety. Save the pills, tinctures, gummies, and teas for when you're super-stressed or coping with a major bout of insomnia.

29. Experiment with Aromatherapy

We often take our sense of smell for granted, but it's a powerful sense that can affect our mood, our memories, and many other aspects of our lives. If you're all macho and you think scents don't matter to you, ask yourself: Why do you buy the brand of deodorant that you buy? Why do you use the hair products you use? Likely, it's because you like their scent.

So, use aromas to your advantage. Many people swear to the anxiety-reducing effects of lavender, and scientific research also points to its anxiolytic (anxiety-reducing) effects. Try washing your clothes and sheets in lavender-scented laundry detergents, or use lavender scent additives when you wash your clothes (the more natural the scent, the better). You can also buy lavender aerosols; spray them in your vicinity when you're feeling nervous or worried. Another good option is to buy a diffuser to disperse lavender essential oils (but be careful where you place the diffuser, as it can leave behind an oily residue).

Note that you can also take herbal supplements that contain lavender; see Tip #28.

30. Write or Journal

Whether you consider yourself a writer or not, writing for just ten or fifteen minutes a day can be extremely therapeutic.

Perhaps you've always wanted to write the Great American Novel, or an idea for a short story has been bouncing around in your head for you can't remember how long. Or you used to keep a journal, but life got in the way, and now journaling seems like a waste of time. Or you like poetry, and you've always wanted to try your hand at it—or maybe write some song lyrics—but you've been intimidated by the idea of getting started.

Scrunch up that trepidation into a tight little ball and toss it into the trashcan. Now pick up your pen, or get to the keyboard, and start. It's incredibly freeing to take pleasure in activity that you know you aren't necessarily good at. When you're writing, you'll likely get into your flow state (see Tip #23), and the hours may fly by as you focus on being creative.

You may find it useful to write about your anxieties or worries. Use paper or your screen as your therapist, and don't worry about spelling or grammar. Typing away on your keyboard is fast and easy, but consider keeping a paper journal. The tactile experience of holding a nice pen (try gel pens—they're great) and writing on a sheet of quality paper in a nicely designed journal can be very relaxing.

If none of these suggestions work for you, find other ways to write. Maybe you have an elderly friend or relative who'd enjoy getting something in the mailbox other than bills and advertisements. Maybe you belong to an organization and would like to contribute a recipe to its newsletter. Maybe you'd like to record family stories for children, nieces, nephews, or grandkids. Now's the time to do it.

31. Spend Time with Pets

The benefits of animal companions are widely documented. Dogs, especially, can pick up on their humans' mood and offer, in their inexplicable way, comfort and calm.

If you decide to buy a pet, carefully consider the breed and its needs. Some breeds are notoriously high strung or have quirks that may drive you crazy instead of calming you. For example, if you're sensitive to noise, the "talking" of a Siamese cat may work against your desire for quiet surroundings. Likewise, some dog breeds' tendency to bark a lot (for example, Shelties) might make the breed not a good match for you.

If you feel that a cat or dog is right for you, consider adopting a rescue animal. Its foster family will have a good understanding of it and will answer your questions truthfully. Older pets come with other benefits, too: They tend to be less energetic and therefore require less playtime. Rescue dogs often come to you pre-house-trained.

Perhaps your schedule won't allow you to care for a pet that requires a lot of maintenance. In that case, try a simple goldfish in a bowl that you keep on your desk. Just watching the goldfish swim around may put bring you to a more tranquil place. Some companies even sell fish tanks with colorful artificial fish that look almost real; you may be amazed by the relaxation induced by the bubbling of a small aquarium.

32. Put Down Your Smart Phone

Have you noticed how many people walk through the supermarket or along the sidewalk with their cell phones in their hands? Amazingly, even adults working out at the gym manage to hold onto their cell phones while they are lifting weights, running on the treadmill, or climbing the StairMaster. Stories are rampant about people who take their phones into the bathroom with them or check them during sex.

Ask yourself: Am I addicted to my phone? If you think the answer might be yes, then you probably are. It all comes down to dopamine, a neurotransmitter (brain chemical) associated with social rewards. Each time you receive an upvote, a thumbs up, a text, a response to a posting, or any other reaction to your online presence, you receive a dopamine jolt, and the more dopamine you get, the more you want.

Is it any surprise, then, that U.S. adults spend an average of two to four hours per day on their mobile phones, which corresponds to touching their phone more than 2,600 times each and every day? In addition, if you've ever lost your phone, you've likely experienced a heightened state of anxiety. In one study, 73% of people reported experiencing exactly that type of anxiety.

If you don't want to experience lost-phone worries or the anxiety that comes when you don't get enough responses or positive reinforcements, causing you to think, "I'm not popular, nobody likes me, people think I'm stupid"?—then there is a simple solution: Disconnect.

It won't be easy, just as giving up cigarettes isn't easy. Turn off notifications, leave the phone in another room, and never sleep in the same room with your phone.

Rather than spending hours on your phone, work on a crossword or jigsaw puzzle, read a book, or have a face-to-face conversation with a friend or co-worker. Leave the phone in your locker when you go to the gym, and never tap on your cell phone while driving. Set a reasonable schedule for yourself. For example, you might begin detaching yourself from your phone by checking it only twelve times during the day, at the same time each hour.

33. Volunteer

Volunteering with an organization that shares your values offers many benefits. While helping you put your anxiety on a shelf as you focus on serving others, it also provides a sense of belonging and fosters a profound gratitude for all your advantages in life. Compared to the challenges facing those you're helping, your worries will likely feel small and insignificant, offering you a valuable change in perspective. Suddenly, your fears and worries seem like tiny bumps in the road rather than huge, overwhelming roadblocks.

No matter where you live, there will be ample opportunities to volunteer. Even if your home is in the middle of a hundred wooded acres, FaceTime, Skype, Zoom, GoogleChats, and a host of other apps allow for face-to-face interaction. Ideally, though, it's best to leave your home to do your volunteer work. At home, worries can fester and multiply, but when you're out of your house and helping others, you'll be so focused on offering comfort and service to others that your own anxieties will recede.

An important tip: Some volunteer organizations are quite political, with volunteers jockeying for notice, high-sounding positions, and decision-making power. Leave such machinations to others, and approach your volunteer work with humility. You're there to help other people, not to take over or steer the ship. Don't get pulled into debates and controversies, and focus on what matters most: your clients.

34. Make Time for Romance—But Cut Yourself Some Slack

If you've already found your ideal romantic partner or life mate, take some time to appreciate that person. But if you haven't, and you're still on the market, you can take a few steps to ensure that your quest for love is an adventure rather than an anxiety-inducing chore.

Although the strict social clock that ruled previous generations has relaxed its stranglehold on humanity a bit, it's still there, ticking in the background: Find someone, get married, buy a house, have children, buy a bigger house … Many single people of all ages spend an enormous chunk of their free time dating, surfing matchmaking apps, meeting this one for coffee, that one for a drink. Dating can feel like another full-time job, and the pressure to date when you're single and all your friends are paired off can feel immense. The result? You may live in a state of perpetual anxiety about your singlehood and the bleak, bleak future you face as an unpaired person.

When it comes to dating, there are two schools of thought: "You need to put yourself out there" and "It'll happen when the time is right." Strive for a balance between the two philosophies. If you sit home on a few Saturday nights, it's not the end of the world. You're not a loser, and you're not pathetic.

Think about what you really want in a mate, and then choose your dates wisely. Only you can define your criteria for the best match, but if you're checking off boxes on a questionnaire, consider selecting all of these:

✓ Calm

✓ Cheerful

✓ Easygoing

✓ Relaxed

Psychological research has shown that most people tend to be attracted to similar people, both in friendships and in romantic relationships, but that doesn't mean that your better half needs to share all of your qualities. You're anxious; wouldn't it be wonderful to have a partner who's calm when you're wired, who's considered when you're a bundle of nerves? The last thing you need in a relationship is someone who's going take his or her own worries and make them yours.

35. Live by the Serenity Prayer

If you've ever been in a gift shop, you've probably seen a plaque featuring the Serenity Prayer, widely attributed to the American theologian Reinhold Niebuhr:

God, grant me the serenity to accept the things I cannot change

courage to change the things I can,

and wisdom to know the difference.

Anxious people often twist their guts, and tie themselves in knots, trying to line everything up in their lives in exactly the order they desire. But other people don't want to be manipulated; nature is by definition uncontrollable; and life is a Major League pitcher that is forever throwing fastballs and curveballs at us.

We have the power to change some things. We can get out of a bad relationship. We can move to a new apartment when our neighbors blast Megadeth at 3 A.M. We can change jobs when we work for a socio/psychopath. When we choose to live with conditions that make us miserable, we keep our anxiety on high boil all the time, and we cede control of our lives to others: to the boyfriend who's always two hours late, to the neighbor who doesn't care that we're sleeping when he wants to listen to death metal, to the boss who would happily split our head open with a hatchet to get a promotion. Making changes in these areas takes courage, but it can be done. In other words, you have the ability to change your situation for the better.

Accepting what you can't change means accepting the world's imperfections. For example: You also have a controlling mother-in-law who hates your guts. You disapprove of the sitting president. You find it frustrating that the shopping malls are so crowded on Saturdays, when you want to do your shopping. You cannot control any of these things, so accept them. If you love your spouse, figure out a way to cope with your mother-in-law. If you despise the president, get your vote on. If you want to shop when the stores aren't crowded, plan to shop on weeknights, an hour before the retail world closes.

In other words: Examine the situation, determine whether you can change it, and act accordingly.

36. Tidy Up

"A messy desk is a sign of genius"—or is it an anxiety attack waiting to happen?

Think about your workspace for a moment. When you look at a desk that looks as if a bomb has exploded on it—when you can't find a pen to write with—when your day planner is buried under mounds of paper—when you can't find the bill you need to pay, or the birthday card you bought for your great aunt Tillie because your desk is covered with books, CDs, notepads, technology, boxes of Cheez-Its, and suchlike—will you ever enter your office and feel a breath of relaxation and tranquility? Likely, you will not.

Messy surroundings aren't comforting. They suggest a lack of organization, an inability to plan, a deficit in keeping up with everyday life. None of these feelings and perceptions are good for your anxiety—and neither is the persistent nagging thought, "I *really* need to clean up around here."

So take some time to de-clutter your life. Haven't used it in a year, and probably will never use it again? Get rid of it. Think you'll need it in six months? Put in a box, label it, and store it in a closet. Free yourself of all the useless paper that you'll never look at again—recycle those newspapers, bills, magazines, catalogues, junk mail. Make the bed as soon as you wake up in the morning so that you can look forward to getting into a freshly made bed at night.

By decluttering your surroundings, you help to declutter your mind.

37. Cover Up the Noise

If you're sensitive to noise, unexpected and unwanted sounds can send you over the edge. The migraine-inducing, high-pitched *beep beep beep* of a truck backing up; the *rat-a-tat-tat* of a woodpecker bent on reducing your house to a pile of sawdust; the muffled *wah-wah-wah* of a too-loud TV in an adjoining apartment; the neighbors' landscapers' *brr-brr-brr* as they blow leaves to edges of the property while you're trying to sleep … None of this racket will help your anxiety.

You may not be able to stop the racket, but you can cover it up by generating alternative noises. It's easier to tune out noise that you've chosen than sounds that are imposed on you. Try playing classical music (no lyrics, so nothing to sing along with) or running a fan at a high speed. The unwanted babel of sounds gets covered up, and you achieve the relaxation that goes with feeling that you have some control over your surroundings.

You can also use a white noise machine to accomplish the same purpose. Some are simple, some are complicated, but all have the same goal: to create a covering sound that will help you relax. Some of the more sophisticated options have dozens of settings, everything from Asian wind chimes, to chirping crickets, to ocean surf, to cosmic pulsations, to gentle spring rain. Many of them are battery-operated and portable, so you can take them with you when you visit relatives or stay in hotels. Ah … portable serenity. What more could you ask for?

38. Indulge in (Reasonable) Retail Therapy

If you're like most people, you may find yourself shopping just for the fun of it. Maybe you go to the local Home Goods or T. J. Maxx and buy a vase you don't really need, or you go on an Internet shopping spree at 2 A.M. Magically, you somehow feel better afterwards. That's not surprising; research has shown that retail therapy can improve your mood.

Nobody is recommending that you become a compulsive shopper (which would trade one set of problems for another), but reasonable retail therapy can be marvelously effective if you use it sparingly and effectively. Here's a way to make it work.

First, set a goal for yourself, such as packing up at least three bags of unused clothes and donating them to a good cause, or getting through a high-stakes presentation for a client. The goal should focus on accomplishing a task that rattles your nerves or otherwise nags at you.

Second, set a budget. Retail therapy doesn't have to cost a lot of money to be effective. If you're on a tight budget, your budget can be just a few dollars. If you have a little more cash to spare, think in terms of a $20 or $25 budget.

Finally, after you've accomplished your goal, set aside some time to splurge. Go to the dollar store and browse, just looking at all the available stuff (and marveling at how much less it costs than it would if you'd purchased it at a supermarket). Or, if your budget is a little higher, spend some time on the Internet, surfing around and keeping track of the items that appeal to you.

Here's the most important part: Don't buy impulsively. If you go to the dollar store, spend at least an hour walking around and looking at the bargains. If you're a catalogue shopper, arrange the catalogues around you and use sticky notes to keep track of pages with intriguing goodies. If you're shopping on the Web, take a couple of hours to surf around, passing the time with free association and click-click-clicking. In walking around the store or browsing the Web, you're distracting yourself from any lingering worries. It's hard to worry when you're looking for that perfect thing to buy.

At the end of the process, you may even find that you don't need to purchase anything because the browsing experience was satisfying enough.

39. Enjoy Comfort Food

Before reading further, please know: This tip is not intended to suggest that you should eat your worries or your emotions. Binge eating, and overeating in general, aren't good coping mechanisms and can have unhealthy results.

But there are times when some good, old-fashioned comfort food can help to distract you for a while. Macaroni and cheese, meatloaf, chili, chicken soup, shepherd's pie, a fast-food burger, French fries—all of them can bring you back to your happy days as a kid, teenager, or young adult.

You get to choose the comfort food that brings you the most comfort. For example, you might try the green Jell-o salad that your grandmother used to make (lime Jell-o, mayonnaise, celery, fruit cocktail) or the Coca-Cola salad (cherries, a can of Coke, black cherry gelatin, pecans, pineapple) that you enjoyed at picnic when you were a child. Or you might indulge in a snack that the food police have deemed evil, such as a chocolate chip muffin.

Whatever your choice, try not to scarf the food. Just sit back and enjoy it. Invite a friend or loved one to join you and agree that calories, fat, cholesterol, salt, and carbs don't matter for this one snack or meal. The goal is pure pleasure, pleasant conversation, laughter, a trip down memory lane, and release from the stresses and anxieties of the day.

40. Calm That Racing Heart

When anxiety kicks into high gear, you may find your heart racing, *thump-thump-thumping* rapidly. Likely the acceleration lasts for only a few seconds, but it feels much longer than that. The racing heart may be a signal that you're about to have a panic attack (see Tip # 56), but in many cases it's just your inborn fight-or-flight reaction responding to a perceived threat that your anxiety has kept alive in your body.

The following is a simple trick to return your racing heart to its normal beat. Take a deep breath and push down on your sphincter, as if you are trying to defecate. Hold the push for a few seconds and then return the muscles to their resting state. Yes, it sounds strange—but it works. By tricking your body into thinking it's about to engage in the natural act of voiding, you re-focus it on an everyday, perfectly natural activity that tamps down the fight-or-flight response.

If your heart starts to race again after a few seconds or minutes of relief, do the exercise a second time and a third time, if necessary. It's like magic: instant relief from those possibly terrifying palpitations.

41. Read a (Printed) Book

If you're a reader, then you already know that reading = relaxation. Many people read just before bed because they know it's the perfect way to move their bodies from awake/aware to ready for sleep.

When you're following an exciting plot, reading about characters you care about, learning something new, or enjoying a book about a favorite hobby, you're focused on being in the moment with that book—not worried about all the things that make you anxious.

If you're not a reader, then give it a try. Here are a few suggestions. First, buy and read a printed book rather than reading on screen. The tactile experience of holding a book and turning the pages is relaxing and pleasing in itself. By reading a printed book, you also get to enjoy the bookmaker's arts, including nicely designed pages with crisp fonts and professionally drawn graphics. Also, getting away from a computer screen will give your fried eyes a break from all the harsh light of the computer in front of which you likely worked all day.

Second, read while lying down or leaning back in a reclining chair, which will position your body for rest.

Last but not least, get rid of all distractions that would diminish your focus or concentration. Turn off the TV, put the phone in another room (and switch it to vibrate), close the door, and immerse yourself in the book you're holding.

If you're not one to read books, then you haven't found the right books to read.

Surf around on Amazon until you find some that appeal to you. Or go to your local

library and ask the staff for recommendations. They'll be glad to help.

42. Turn the Camera Away from Yourself

Modern technology has built remarkable cameras into our smart phones. The result has been a barrage of gorgeous photography from everywhere in the world.

But there's a dark side to carrying an easy-to-use camera with you everywhere you go: selfies, which can cause you to become more interested in recording the moment rather than living it. Even more troubling is the concern with looking with looking perfect in the selfies that you take. Check out almost any person's camera roll and you'll see dozens of versions of the same picture. Why so many? The selfie-taker wanted many, many photos so that s/he could choose the "perfect" version to post on social media.

Human beings aren't perfect, but selfies suggest that they can be, as long as they take enough photos to ensure that they get the ideal lighting, perfect posture, and more pleasing facial expression. Underneath the anxiety is our fear that the world won't accept us unless our stomachs are flat, our teeth pearly whites, our complexions smooth and blemish-free, our backdrop that of a Renaissance painting. The pressure to be perfect already plagues people who suffer with anxiety; do we really need more pressure to create flawless images of ourselves?

There's nothing wrong with posing for photos with friends and family. But think twice before you take that next series of selfies. As yourself: Why am I taking this photo? Who is going to see it, and why do I care what that person thinks? What can I do instead to be happy in the moment?

43. Break the Cycle of Negative Thinking

Psychologist Aaron Beck developed an important theory regarding depression, identifying to a "negative triad" of dysfunctional beliefs that can lead to difficulties in coping with everyday life. The triad includes negative and inaccurate beliefs with respect to three categories:

- The self: "I'm unlovable," "I'm unattractive and nobody likes me," "I'm too dumb to figure this out."
- The world: "Other people exclude me from their activities," "There's no justice in the world," "The system is preventing me from being successful."
- The future: "We'll never recover from this recession," "The future of humanity is bleak," "I'm going to be poor and lonely in retirement."

An effective means of battling anxiety is to challenge the dark triad, to pull apart such thoughts and recognize how illogical and inaccurate they are. Beck developed a type of therapy called cognitive therapy to help patients identify their negative thought habits and then re-orient their thinking. If you are prone to doomsday thinking, and you have difficulty pulling yourself away from such unpleasant thoughts even when you're aware of them, you might try seeking out a therapist. Cognitive behavioral therapy has proven quite effective at treating anxiety (see Tip #99).

44. Perform a Random Act of Kindness

A random act of kindness is an unexpected, positive action that you perform for a stranger. People performing random acts of kindness have paid for the fast food of the strangers in the car behind them at the drive-thru; have left Starbucks gift cards on the windshields of strangers' cars in parking lots; have left care packages of crayons and art supplies for teachers in underfunded schools. The possibilities are endless.

The idea of performing random acts of kindness first caught on in the early 1990s. As anyone who's ever performed such an act can tell you, the feeling of warmth and shared humanity that it generates is enormous. If you've ever been on the receiving end of such an act, you likely felt a profound sense of connection with the stranger who'd done something unexpectedly kind for you.

People who suffer with anxiety are often consumed with the perceived challenges in their lives. They are so focused on worrying about their own problems that they fail to acknowledge their blessings. By thinking about the small ways that you can bring a bit of joy to someone else, you shift your thinking. In doing so, you become the provider of someone else's happiness rather than a worrier about your own.

Try it, and if you get "caught in the act," explain that you're just trying to pay it forward, which will likely encourage the other person to do the same.

45. Write a Positive Review

One of the Internet's great contributions is its ability to make different voices heard. You may wonder whether people care about your opinion. They do, especially when they are making purchase decisions.

The Internet is loaded with sites that allow you to review and rate just about anything—Goodreads for books, TripAdvisor for hotels and other accommodations, Yelp for restaurants and other public venues, IMDB for movies, and many more.

If you've enjoyed a book, film, restaurant, or any other experience, you have the opportunity to pay it forward by leaving a favorable review. Explain why you enjoyed the experience by providing specific details. Note the specific reasons for your pleasure, complimenting (for example) the writing, the plot, a specific employee's performance, a particularly delicious entrée, or an exceptional experience with customer service. Small business owners really benefit from such reviews, and all types of artists—from writers to musicians to actors to dancers to painters and sculptors—need such feedback in a world in which they are relentlessly criticized.

Just as important, you benefit from writing a glowing review. By sitting down and taking the time to think about a positive experience, you think deeply about something that brought you pleasure. Your anxiety will lessen as you emphasize the positive instead of dwelling on the negative.

A note: If you've had a bad experience with a business, contact the owners or managers rather than leave a bad review that could destroy everything they've worked to build. That's a more positive way of dealing with the situation, and you'll likely be pleased with the outcome.

46. Get a New Alarm Clock

Many people don't realize that they start their day in the most unpleasant way imaginable, with the annoying buzzing, beeping, or ringing of an insistent alarm clock. The problem is compounded if your anxiety makes sleep difficult to begin with. You feel as though you've just succeeded in nodding off, and then there it is—that miserable cacophony signaling that it's 6:30 A.M. and you need to get out of bed whether you want to or not.

There's a much better way to wake up: a gentle alarm clock.

They come in all shapes and sizes, and they use different methods to wake you from your slumbers mildly. Some use light, while others use vibration. Still others use gentle sounds, such as chirping crickets or a babbling brook. Often the sounds start at very low volume and then get progressively louder, though never loud enough to become obnoxious. A clock that uses aromas to move you from sleep to wakefulness can be a godsend if you respond well to pleasant scents, such as lemon or orange.

For many people, getting out of bed will never be fun, but it's so much easier when you're not jolted awake by the equivalent of an air-raid siren. Your bed and bedroom should be a sanctuary, so don't let a shrieking alarm clock disturb your inner sanctum. Start each new day afresh with a sound (or light or aroma) that soothes your anxiety instead of kick-starting it as soon your eyes pop open.

47. Avoid Your Triggers

The daily occurrences that trigger anxiety vary from person to person. What people, situations, activities, and events ratchet up your anxiety? Maybe your heart skips a beat when you see that stuck-up neighbor on her way to regale you with tales of her perfect children. Or the thought of making a presentation to a roomful of colleagues makes your heart start thumping. Or you know an ex is going to be at the same dinner party to which you've been invited, and you just don't want to deal with it.

Nobody knows better than you what those triggers are, so take a few minutes to write down your personal list of anxiety triggers. Once you know your triggers, you can come up with solutions for avoiding them. It's not realistic to expect that you can completely eliminate triggers from your life, but you can certainly reduce them. That stuck-up neighbor? Look out of your window before leaving the house to make sure she's nowhere in sight; or, if you must leave the house, pretend that you're talking on your cell phone and give her a quick wave. That anxiety-producing presentation? Make sure you've practiced, and make sure that a friend or supporter is present during the presentation. The dinner party? Send your regrets.

Avoiding your triggers is just one aspect of making choices that bring you happiness rather than upset. You have the right to manage your life, to avoid situations that make you unhappy. One word of caution, though: Make sure you're not avoiding important things, such as going to your kids' parent-teacher meetings or attending business meetings that are important for your career. To manage anxiety in those situations, use the other tips in this book.

48. Allow Yourself a Worry Period

Has anyone ever said to you, "Don't think about a pink elephant"? If so, then the first thing you thought of was, most likely, a pink elephant. The mere suggestion put that pink pachyderm at the forefront of your consciousness.

You may have had a similar experience when a friend, significant other, or co-worker ordered you to "stop worrying" or more gently suggested, "There's nothing to worry about." Now, in addition to worrying about whatever it is that's concerning you, you have to worry that you're annoying or upsetting people with your worry.

Few of us will ever be completely free of anxiety, so don't set yourself up for failure by thinking, "Within three months, I will be a completely carefree, light-hearted person. I will tiptoe through the tulips without a care in the world." Instead, control your anxiety by allowing yourself a worry period each day. Set aside 10 to 15 minutes to think about, write about, or talk about your worries, because acknowledging them is the first important step in managing and lessening them. Then, throughout the day as your worries creep into your thoughts, tell yourself, like Scarlett O'Hara, that tomorrow is another day, and you'll worry about X, Y, and Z during tomorrow's worry period.

49. Develop an Anti-Anxiety Alliance

Do you have someone in your life whose anxiety level is similar to yours? Try setting up an Anti-Anxiety Alliance with that person.

Many of the twelve-step programs partner their members with another member of the group. The idea is that almost everyone can benefit from having a person to turn to when the going gets rough. You can adapt this idea by making a pact with a fellow anxiety-sufferer. Here's how it works:

You both agree to talk each other down off the ledge when the other is feeling anxious. So, for example, let's say you're worried about your bills and your job. You call your partner to worry out loud. Your partner responds with soothing words and helps you brainstorm solutions, which has the additional benefit of helping that person cope better when he or she encounters similar challenges.

An Anti-Anxiety Alliance works only when both people can promise to remain relentlessly positive in the face of the other person's worries. As we've seen earlier (Tip #18), we sometimes find ourselves around other people who chief goal in life seems to be working us into a frenzy. The goal here is to find someone who's as devoted to reducing his or her anxiety as you are.

50. Drink Chamomile Tea

Chamomile tea is widely believed to have relaxing properties, and scientific research has pointed to its effectiveness as an anxiolytic (a substance that reduces anxiety). It has no caffeine, which makes it the perfect nighttime beverage if you're the type of person who likes to drink warm beverages after dinner or even before bed. An additional benefit is the comfort of holding a warm mug in your hands, which is relaxing in itself.

Chamomile can be a bit of an acquired taste, so you can feel free to sweeten it with a bit of local honey, which many people believe to have potent antiviral effects. Don't overdo it with the sweetener, though, especially at nighttime.

You can also make large batches of chamomile tea, adding some sweetener, and keeping it in the refrigerator instead of drinking prepackaged, high-sugar iced teas. Many yummy flavors of nondairy creamer are available to add to your iced chamomile tea, from Italian Sweet Cream, to Caramel Macchiato, to Almond Joy, to Butterscotch, to Double Chocolate—and the calorie count per serving is usually quite reasonable.

51. Just Say No

Many people are reluctant to say the simple word "No." They don't have the time or the desire to help with that bake sale, play that round of golf when they'd rather be sleeping, or take that road trip that will put them behind on everything else in their life, but they say "Yes." Then they regret it almost immediately as their stress and anxiety levels rise.

Saying No doesn't make you a rude or selfish person. It makes you a person who manages your commitments, and your anxiety, by granting you the freedom to make the decisions that will help you manage your life and your schedule.

There are many ways to say No:

- "I'd like to, but I just don't have the time right now."

- "Can I take a rain check? I'm juggling a lot."

- "Darn. I have a work thing on that day that I can't get out of." (Whether true or not.)

- "That's just not something I enjoy doing any more."

- "My workload is very heavy as it is. I can't take on anything else right now without the quality of my work slipping."

Note that none of these sentences offers an apology. You don't need to apologize for not being interested in or not having the time to perform the requested task or accept the proffered invitation. Just be careful about not saying No too often. If you do, the invitations may stop coming.

52. Chew Gum

Some experts suggest that chewing gum can help to relieve anxiety. The blood flow to your brain increases when you chew gum, decreasing your level of stress and increasing your sense of well-being. Stronger chewing may lead to even greater stress relief.

Although it may be tough to believe that an act as simple as masticating may offer some relief from anxiety, it makes sense at a basic biological level. When your anxiety is in high gear, your flight-or-right response is active, and your body is revved up. Chewing on a wad of gum gives your body something to do, an activity to focus on. When you're focused on a physical act such as chewing something and remembering not to swallow it, you're diverting your thoughts and your body from attending to the signals that would increase or maintain your anxiety.

An added bonus: You'll have sweet-smelling, fresh breath.

53. Train Away Distorted Thought Patterns

Many college instructors train students how to think critically—that is, to evaluate whether information is logical and accurate. Using examples from the media, they explain how to identify common logical fallacies that reveal bias or flawed reasoning and argumentation. Some of those fallacies are the bandwagon fallacy ("Everyone's doing it, so it must be good"), either-or reasoning ("Either you're with us or against us"), the slippery slope ("If we tax the wealthy, they'll stop spending money, and our world economy will be destroyed"), and hasty generalization ("Political Party X stands for the common people, while Political Party Y is all about power and money").

Logical fallacies have their emotional equivalent in the types of distorted thinking that plague those who live with anxiety. It is therefore helpful to recognize and correct any tendency to think in ways that maintain or increase your anxiety. Specifically, be on the lookout for the following types of thinking.

- All-or-nothing thinking, in which you view the world in black and white without seeing the shades of gray: "If I don't get a perfect performance review, I'll get fired."
- Disqualifying the positive, in which you acknowledge positive experiences but then discount them: "I hit a home run, but that was a fluke. I'll never do it again."
- Emotional reasoning, in which you base conclusions on an emotional hunch: "I sense that she doesn't like me, so therefore it must be true."

- Fortune telling, in which you reach sweeping conclusions based on limited experience: "My book was rejected by two publishers, so it'll never get published."

- Mind reading, in which you think you know what another person is thinking: "She thinks I'm not a good mother."

- Overgeneralizing, in which you base a conclusion on very few experiences or interactions: "All the people who work here are just out for themselves."

- Personalizing, in which you take on all the responsibility for an outcome: "My team lost the game because I had a cold and I wasn't playing at my best."

- "Shoulding all over yourself," in which you set unrealistic expectations for yourself that you can never meet, often by using the word *should*, *must*, or *need*: "I need to be the best parent in my neighborhood," "I should go that family reunion," "I must lose ten pounds by the end of the month."

When you find yourself in a negative thought loop, immediately distract yourself. Do something with your hands that requires your concentration, or sing along to a favorite song. After you break the loop (it may take several tries), you can go back and re-examine your thinking, coming up with a list of reasons why a certain thought makes no sense when you examine it logically and objectively.

54. Practice Gratitude

It's easy to feel anxiety in a world that tells us, both subtly and overtly, that we don't have enough—not enough friends, not enough money, not enough things. Our achievements, our emotional states, and our core being can be eclipsed by the long shadow of want. We may think we want and need more even though we may be quite satisfied (although not perfectly satisfied) with our current situation.

The pressure to have and want more, more, more can chain you to a treadmill that keeps you trapped in a cycle of anxiety and worry. The more you have, the more you want … Otherwise, why do Warren Buffett, Mark Zuckerberg, and Jeff Bezos continue to go to work everyday? They are the Masters of the Universe, to borrow a line from Tom Wolfe. You are not Warren, Mark, or Jeff. You are you: a person who's responsible for finding your own happiness with the resources at your disposal.

Rather than lust for that expensive handbag, fancy watch, or McMansion that's way beyond your financial comfort zone, take the time to be grateful for what you have: health, a family, a stable job, a roof over your head, a rewarding hobby, a good friend. By choosing to focus on your blessings and your achievements, you step off the treadmill, your heart rate returns to normal, and your anxiety lessens.

55. Take a Staycation

Many of us live by an unforgiving schedule: Get up at a specific time, go to work, run errands, go to the gym, get home, do chores, pay the bills, catch up on X, Y, and Z over the weekend. We have almost no unscheduled down time.

A staycation, in which you take vacation time from work but don't go anywhere or do anything, can be a wonderful gift to yourself. Rather than going through the day with the clock ticking off the minutes until you're due at the next meeting, you get to choose what you want to do and, just as importantly, what you don't want to do. A staycation is like a day at the beach, but without the crowds, the sunburn, the traffic, and the overpriced food on the boardwalk.

The guidelines for a successful staycation are simple. First, don't make any plans in advance. Take it one day at a time. Feel like sleeping in? Then stay in your bed until you're ready to get out of it. Feel like getting up early to go for a run? Set the alarm and have your running gear ready to be donned when you wake up. Want to spend the whole day reading? Then read to your heart's content. Feel like fishing? Grab your gear and make for the nearest lake or pond. Want to do something you haven't done since you were a kid, such as go miniature golfing? Then do it. It's your staycation—you get to make the rules.

Freedom from obligations and responsibilities, if only for a short time, is extremely relaxing, and it can help you view everyday errands or annoyances in a different light. For example, when you're pressed for time during the week, going to the bank can feel like a time-wasting hassle. When you're indulging in a week of staying at home, that same errand can feel like a moderately enjoyable short road trip.

84

56. Manage a Panic Attack

Sweating palms. Racing heart. Trembling hands. Hyperventilation. The fear that you're having a heart attack or stroke. Anyone who's experienced a panic attack will recognize these extremely unpleasant symptoms, often accompanied by the sense of imminent death.

The key to managing an anxiety attack is to recognize it as it's coming on. When you start to shake uncontrollably and your mind starts to spin out of control, it's time to control your breathing. Some people find it helpful to breathe in and out deeply into a paper bag, but the bag itself isn't what's important here. Rather, it's the focus on taking slow, deep breaths that distract your mind from its racing anxiety. Many people find the square breathing or box breathing method effective: Begin by exhaling through your mouth to empty the air from your lungs. Next, inhale slowly and deeply through your nose for a count of four, feeling the air fill your lungs. Then hold your breath for a count of four. Finally, exhale slowly for a count of four. Repeat as many times as necessary.

You may also find it helpful to close your eyes as you breathe; doing so can help you eliminate distractions. Another option is to focus on a particular object as you breathe, or to imagine a calm place where you've felt relaxed and happy, such as a beach or a mountain retreat.

Above all else, remember that you aren't dying. You're having a panic attack, and you're dealing with it. Just knowing that you can control a panic attack may cause you to have fewer panic attacks in the future.

If you suffer anxiety attacks regularly, see your doctor.

57. Avoid Procrastination

Are the unanswered e-mails piling up? Have you put off weeding the yard so long that your home is starting to look like the Munsters'? Each time you sat down to begin writing that report, did you find yourself compelled to do unnecessary household chores instead? Have you been putting off a difficult conversation that you really must have? Is your mantra, "Why do it today when it can wait until tomorrow, or the next day, or the day after that?"

Procrastination has many causes, among them a fear of failure, concern about the aftermath of the dreaded or undesirable activity, and an inability to focus, often because you're too distracted by your technology to attend to anything else.

We all put off doing things from time to time, and occasional procrastination is nothing to be concerned about. But if you procrastinate regularly, ask yourself: Does my anxiety level rise with each day that I put off that important task or conversation, because procrastination allows my stress and worry to build up?

You can use a few simple techniques to get ahead of procrastination. First, identify what you need to do, breaking the task down into smaller chunks. Then start on it, even if your start-up time is only five or ten minutes. Devote a specific amount of time each day toward completing your task. (A half an hour is a good starting point.) Work on your task in an environment that's conducive to concentration, and eliminate all distractions (TV, cell phone, music). You may find yourself getting into a flow state (see Tip #23) and making unexpected, substantial progress toward your goal. Reward yourself for reaching certain milestones that you established at the start of the project, with the biggest reward coming when you've finished.

Finally, don't beat yourself up for having procrastinated in the past. Research suggests that the more slack you can cut yourself for putting things off in the past, the better the odds of avoiding it in the future.

58. Stand Up Straight and Tall

Your posture can not only reflect your anxiety but also add to it. Tamar Chansky, author of *Freeing Yourself from Anxiety*, notes that when we are anxious, we protect our upper body—the location of our heart and lungs—by hunching over. To relieve your anxiety, she recommends that you stand on your two feet with your legs widely apart, balance your weight evenly, stand tall, pull your shoulders back, open your chest, and breathe deeply.

By assuming a standing, confident posture that enables deep breathing, you enlist your body's aid in reducing anxiety. Here, as in so many of the other tips in this book, deep, invigorating, stress-releasing breathing is key.

59. Avoid Judgment—Practice Compassion

It's easy to sit in an observer's seat and criticize the world. Certainly there's a lot to be critical about: overpaid and overexposed celebrities; the norming of plastic surgery that makes people look like mannequins, or space aliens; the inanity of much social media; politicians at the local, state, and national scale. For those who view the world through a negative lens, the opportunities for critical judgments are endless.

But when you're fixated on pointing out the world's problems, you stay on high alert for opportunities to criticize. Your nerves are always tingling as you work yourself up about this, that, or the other thing. Focusing on what's wrong in the world only makes you feel worse about it.

Avoid judgment and try compassion instead. For example, rather than demonize the members of a political party, try to understand why they think and vote as they do. Rather than becoming annoyed by a braggart, try to see and empathize with the insecure person within. Rather than scream about no-talent celebrities who make way too much money, ask yourself how you'd feel about living with the many challenges of being a celebrity, such as a complete lack of privacy and the dire necessity to look perfect in order to keep working.

Like random acts of kindness (see Tip #44), compassion brings good to the world and relief from some of your anxiety.

60. Choose Your Colors

You likely carefully chose the colors for each room in your home. Perhaps your breakfast nook is a cheerful yellow to help you wake up. Your little girl's room may have pink walls, and your home office may be a more serious affair with a lot of dark wood and brown tones.

Color can have a powerful effect on mood, energizing you or relaxing you, making you feel comfortable or uncomfortable. For example, red increases the stress response, but white and green do not.

A recent study by the British papermaker G.F. Smith, conducted with the University of Sussex in Brighton, England, has identified blue—especially navy blue—as the most relaxing color in the world. One of the researchers suggests that humans associate dark blue with sleeping and rest because it is the color of many natural landscapes, such as the nighttime sky and the open seas. In second and third place were turquoise/teal and pastel pink.

How can you make blue work for you? Consider painting your bedroom, office, den, or sanctuary (see Tip #22) a warm, pleasing blue. The options are almost infinite; at your local paint retailer, you'll find more variations on navy blue than you ever thought possible. When you're done painting, let the calming blue wash over you and sweep some of your anxieties away.

61. Go 21 Days Without Complaining

Will Bowen, a minister in Kansas City, Missouri, is on a mission. He wants everyone to go three weeks without complaining for the simple reason that complaining doesn't work.

The task is simple: Stop complaining immediately, and don't let a single complaint escape your lips for the next 21 days. If you complain, you have to start all over again from Day 1.

As Bowen reports, many people rise to his 21-day challenge are surprised by their almost constant complaining. Those same people are then amazed by the positive changes that result from a cessation of criticism and faultfinding. Their spirits feel lighter, they accept and feel compassion for others (see Tip #59), and they make a positive difference in the world.

If you suffer from anxiety, you may think that complaining helps you vent your feelings. But ask yourself: Does complaining actually accomplish anything? Do you really feel any better after letting loose a litany of protests? Most likely, you do not. Instead, you remain stuck at the same place you began.

According to Bowen, a good place to begin your efforts to stop complaining is to use a different set of words:

Instead of ...	*Try* ...
Problem	Opportunity
Have to	Get to
Setback	Challenge
Enemy	Friend
Tormentor	Teacher
Pain	Signal
I demand	I would appreciate
Struggle	Journey
You did this	I created this

Source: Bowen, p. 105.

Give it a try, and see if your anxiety diminishes along with your complaints.

62. Limit Alcohol and Quit Smoking

A beer, a glass of wine, a shot of whisky, a cigarette—all are time-honored traditions for attempting to cope with stress and anxiety. It's not surprising, then that the total volume of alcohol consumed in the world has risen a whopping a 70% over the past three decades. In the United States alone, alcohol consumption has risen 5.4% since 2010, and one study has shown that 73% of the adult U.S. population now drinks alcohol.

Fortunately, the percentage of U.S. adults who smoke cigarettes has declined, from 20.9% in 2005 to 13.7% in 2018, but that's still 243 million adult Americans who smoke.

Using alcohol and/or tobacco to manage your anxiety is like using aerosol air fresheners: They cover up the problem for a while, but they don't address the source. And the negative effects of alcohol and tobacco are well documented: Alcohol use can lead to Type 2 diabetes, high blood pressure, cirrhosis of the liver, and stroke. Smoking is a leading cause of the particularly painful and fatal lung cancer.

If you smoke, make a promise to yourself that you'll stop. (And think of all the money you'll save.) If you like an occasional drink, that's fine. Moderate drinking, which means one drink per day for healthy women and two drinks per day for healthy men, is generally considered safe. But if you find yourself drinking more than moderately to cope with your anxiety, it's time to find other solutions. This book provides 100 of them!

63. Leave Work at Work

Does you work–life balance stink? If so, you're not alone. Beginning with outsourcing and offshoring in the 1980s, continuing through the moderate recessions of the 1990s, and continuing with blazing force through the Great Recession of 2007-2009 and the COVID-19 pandemic, employers have been finding any conceivable excuse to eliminate and automate positions. When they can't do that, they shift work to the Philippines and other countries with ultra-low labor costs. Millions of qualified, experienced, decently paid U.S. workers have been laid off in an effort to "trim costs" (read: increase profits). For the lucky few who remain, the message is: If you don't like your job, there are plenty of people who will do it for a lot less money.

Is it any wonder that so many workers work seven-day weeks, often late into the night? They check email obsessively, fearful of missing an important message or appearing less than 100% dedicated to their employer. Job insecurity also leads to truly vicious office politics that can send anxiety levels skyrocketing.

It's probably not realistic to say, "Quit your job and find one that doesn't demand every minute of your time," because very few such jobs exist. But you *can* draw a dividing line between your life and work. Leave the politics at the office; don't bring them home with you. If you work from home, set up a separate space that is the only place in which you conduct business. Make the hours between 9 P.M. and 8 A.M. an email no-fly zone: Don't check or respond to email during those hours.

If you have to work on weekends, choose a few hours to work and then get an early start on Monday morning. Also identify the many different ways you can appear to be working while not actually working. "The Internet was down," "The cable company was working on the line," and "My machine got a virus" can all work in a pinch.

64. Listen to the Most Relaxing Song in the World

"Music has charms to soothe a savage breast / To soften rocks, or bend a knotted oak," according to the English poet and playwright William Congreve ("The Mourning Bride," 1697).

To soothe your own anxiety, you might trying listening to the song that has been called the most relaxing song in the world: "Weightless," by Marconi Union. Working with sound therapists, Marconi Union set out to use rhythm, bass, and harmonies to decrease listeners' blood pressure, stress hormones, and heart rate. In one research study, listening to "Weightless" decreased participants' overall anxiety by 65 percent.

Dr. David Lewis-Hodgson, the lead researcher, noted, "'Weightless' was so effective, many women became drowsy and I would advise against driving while listening to the song because it could be dangerous."

You can find the song, along with a 10-hour extended version of it, on YouTube. (Better yet, buy the track from iTunes so that the musicians receive some compensation.)

Inc. online lists nine additional tracks to relax (but not to drive) by:

- "We Can Fly," by Rue du Soleil (Café del Mar)
- "Canzonetta Sull'aria," by Mozart
- "Someone Like You," by Adele
- "Pure Shores," by All Saints
- "Please Don't Go," by Barcelona
- "Strawberry Swing," by Coldplay

- "Watermark," by Enya

- "Mellomaniac (Chill Out Mix)," by DJ Shah

- "Electra," by Airstream

Also try two superb, relaxing albums by The Blue Nile: *Hats* and *Peace at Last*.

- "Watermark," by Enya

- "Mellomaniac (Chill Out Mix)," by DJ Shah

- "Electra," by Airstream

65. Don't Catastrophize

I'm running five minutes late for work—I'll definitely get fired.

My closest friend didn't answer my text—She's ghosting me.

My teenager has been moody—He has a serious problem and needs to be medicated.

My car is making a strange noise—The repair's going to cost thousands that I don't have, and without a car I won't be able to get to work, and without work I'll get thrown out of my apartment, and without an apartment I'll end up leaving on the streets and eating garbage …

Catastrophizing means viewing or presenting a situation as considerably worse than it is. It turns small, manageable problems into huge, snarling beasts. In reality:

You probably won't get fired if you're not chronically late.

Your friend has been busy and will text you back when she gets a minute.

Your teenager is being a teenager.

Your car needs some work, perhaps expensive, perhaps inexpensive. You won't know for sure until you talk with a qualified mechanic.

When your mind moves toward the worst-case scenario, keep yourself from sliding down that slippery slope. Halt the downward spiral of your thoughts, and take action to reduce your anxiety. Call the office and explain why you'll be a few minutes late. Wait a day or so and text your friend to check in. Read books about effective ways to parent a cranky teen. Develop a relationship with a mechanic you trust.

66. Develop an Internal Locus of Control

Does the world control your destiny, or are you in charge of your own life? Do you think "Why do these things happen to me?—or do you think "This isn't great; what can I do to make the situation better?"

The psychological term *locus of control* refers to your belief system regarding the factors that contribute to your success or failure. If you have an *external* locus of control, you attribute the events of your life to chance, luck, or circumstances beyond your control. If you have an *internal* locus of control, you see your success or failure as the result of your own abilities, efforts, and actions. Research over the course of several decades has suggested that people with an external locus of control tend to be more prone to anxiety and depression.

If you tend to focus on external events as the sources of the challenges in your life, you can develop a more internal locus of control by focusing on a few key thoughts and behaviors. First, recognize that, in most cases, you have choices. Second, avoid negative self-talk and self-defeating beliefs (see Tips #17, #43, and #53). Third, recognize that you may not always be able to affect what happens, but you can choose how to respond. Fourth, identify a person in your life who has an internal locus of control. What can you learn from him or her? Finally, focus on solutions rather than symptoms.

Remember: You *do* have the power to change the sources of stress and anxiety in your life.

67. Get Enough Light Early in the Day

You probably don't need to be convinced of light's emotional power. When you wake up to a cold, rainy, cloudy day, don't you want to stay in bed? In contrast, when you wake up to bright sunlight and a blazing blue sky, don't you start the day with more energy, more verve, more pizzazz, more motivation to get through your to-do list?

Light therapy, sometimes called phototherapy, is often used to treat people who suffer from seasonal affective disorder (SAD), a common diagnosis for people who are mentally healthy for most of the year but who exhibit symptoms of depression during a specific season, usually winter. Psychologists believe the lack of daylight during the winter disrupts our bodies' natural rhythms, causing increased responses to anxiety- and stress-inducing events.

During light therapy, you sit or work near a box that simulates natural light or gives off bright light. The light is believed to have a positive effect on brain chemicals that affect mood and sleep. Light therapy has proved quite effective in treating SAD and depression, but scientific evidence also suggests that it can also help people who suffer from anxiety.

Light therapy usually works best when it's done in the morning. Because light therapy is intended to help restore your body's natural circadian rhythms, you don't want to expose yourself to bright light in the evening or at night before bed. Light therapy boxes are available on the Internet for very reasonable prices, but it's important to talk with your doctor about the proper way to use them. (For example, you should never stare into the light bulb.)

68. Take Your Vitamins

Very few large-scale studies of vitamin efficacy have been done, but some research suggests that the following vitamins can be useful in lessening anxiety:

- Fish oil
- Magnesium
- Vitamin A
- Vitamin B
- Vitamin C
- Vitamin E

Ask your doctor whether taking any of these vitamins, singly or in combination, might help decrease your anxiety.

69. Talk with a Licensed Therapist

Sigmund Freud invented the term "talking cure" to emphasize the role of talk in the treatment of psychological disorders. Though much of Freud's work has been discredited, the idea of a talking cure has firmly taken root in our society. Today, there are more than 577,000 mental health professionals working in the United States.

The tips in this book have focused on steps that you can take to reduce your anxiety. If you continue to struggle, consider talking with a licensed therapist. Two tried-and-true psychological techniques for treating anxiety are cognitive behavioral therapy and exposure therapy. Cognitive behavioral therapy (CBT) teaches you to examine your own negative thoughts, how to challenge them, and how to replace them with realistic or affirming thoughts. (See Tip #99.) Exposure therapy exposes you, a little bit a time, to items or situations that provoke anxiety. The underlying idea is that when you feel more control over a situation, your anxiety will diminish.

With video messaging and doctor-on-demand services now widely available, more people than ever have access to licensed mental health professionals, and you may be able to receive the help you need without leaving your home.

70. Ask Your Doctor About Anti-Anxiety Medication

You may have noticed that, up until this point, this book hasn't even mentioned the word *medication.* But when all else fails, medicine may help.

Anti-anxiety medications, called anxiolytics, have helped millions of people find relief from debilitating anxiety. Each medicine has its pros, cons, and potential side effects.

Although family doctors and general practitioners can prescribe anti-anxiety medication, it is best to seek the advice of a psychiatrist, who is a medical doctor specializing in psychological diagnosis, treatment, and care. He or she may ask you to try different medications, or different combinations of treatments, until you find what works best for you.

If your doctor prescribes a medication, be sure to read all of the information that comes with it, and closely monitor your reactions. Does it make you sleepy? Groggy? Aggressive? Discussing the reactions with your doctor will be essential in helping you find the right treatment.

Part II: The Specifics

In Part I, we provided 70 different methods of dealing with general anxieties. In this section, we offer tips for managing some of the most common specific anxieties, such as those related to money, family, travel, and the workplace.

71. Take Control of Your Money by Managing Your Spending

The mortgage. The kids' college tuition. Medical coverage and healthcare. Utilities, car insurance, home insurance. Groceries that seem to cost more each time you visit the supermarket. It's no wonder that Americans are swimming in debt. In 2019, U.S. consumer debt topped $14 trillion, a number that will grow significantly as a result of the COVID-19 virus that shut down the world economy for several months in 2020.

It's not surprising, then, that money is a nearly constant source of stress and anxiety for so many people. Here are ten steps you can take to spend less—and therefore worry less about having the money to pay your bills.

1. Don't spend more than you earn. It's as simple as that. If you're not a millionaire, don't live like one. The key to long-term financial comfort is living beneath your means, not at or above them.

2. Pay off your credit card in full each month. Credit-card companies charge astronomical interest rates. If you make only the minimum payment on a fairly large balance, you could end up paying tens of thousands of dollars in interest. So use your credit card for the convenience and the rewards, but don't use it to finance things you can't afford.

3. Make saving a priority. Plan to save a minimum of 10% of your pay, and keep that money strictly off limits. Use it for emergencies only. (Wanting a new car is not an emergency. Needing a new septic system is.) Take advantage of your employers' 401(k) match to save for retirement. Leaving the match on the table is like lighting a match to $1,000 bills.

4. Don't pay for your children's education. Many parents use their retirement savings to pay for their college-age children's tuition, room, and board. College students who must pay their own way often make better decisions in terms of what they can afford: for example, the quality state university compared to, say, Columbia University (2019-2020 tuition and fees: $61,850), Trinity College ($59,050), Tufts University ($58,578), or Kenyon College ($58,570).

5. Don't buy more house than you can afford. Think twice if you have to "stretch" to buy that house or expensive apartment that you fell in love with. In addition to a stressful mortgage, you'll have higher property taxes, higher utility bills, higher landscaping bills (if you don't do the yard work yourself), and higher repair costs.

6. Hunt for bargains. Whatever you want to buy—you can most likely find it for a better price somewhere else. Negotiate prices, and don't be afraid to walk away. Whatever it is, you don't need it so badly that you should overpay for it.

7. Cook at home. If you're having money problems, stop eating at restaurants and stop ordering take-out. You can save an enormous amount of money by shopping sales at the supermarket and cooking at home.

8. Don't turn your nose up at hand-me-downs. Infants outgrow their clothes quickly. Do you really need to spend hundreds or thousands of dollars on new clothes when your siblings, cousins, and friends likely have all the clothes and baby paraphernalia (such as cribs and playpens) that you'll ever need?

9. Lose your taste for new cars. Today's cars are so well built that they can easily go ten years and 200,000 miles. Many people spend enormous amounts of money trading in their car every few years for a newer, fancier, more ostentatious model. Look at your car as investment: If you maintain it well, it'll pay you back with ten years of transportation at a fraction of the what you'd pay to support a new-car habit.

10. Spend wisely. It makes good sense to purchase quality appliances and furniture. It makes no sense to spend $1,000 for a pair of shoes, $3,500 for a men's suit, or $2,000 for a woman's handbag. Buy Prada, Gucci, Louis Vuitton, and Rolex only if you're a millionaire. If you need to keep up with the Joneses, see Tip #20.

72. Obsess Less About Your Kids

The two most difficult jobs in the world are being a spouse and being a parent. Of the two, being a parent is probably the bigger challenge. Kids have a way of doing exactly what we don't want them to, choosing careers that are different from those that we've selected for them, and dating (and perhaps marrying) people who don't meet our standards.

Excessive worry about your children isn't good for you, and it certainly isn't good for them, either. Here are some suggestions for managing your anxiety by worrying less about your kids throughout their lifespan.

1. Remember: Every child is unique. Some children walk and talk sooner than others. Some make friends more easily. Don't panic when your infant isn't speaking while your neighbor's kid is saying "dada," or when little Suzie is potty-trained but yours is still in diapers.

2. Monitor but don't interfere in friendships. At some point, your child will have a friend you don't like. Unless you perceive a real threat to your child, stay out of it, and don't work yourself into a frenzy. Eventually, children learn to break up unfulfilling friendships.

3. Teach your children how to cope with hurt and disappointment. You can try to protect your children from the world, but sooner or later adversity will strike. Teaching your children to cope with adversity will serve them well in the long run. Coddling them and training them that the world will accommodate their every need won't.

4. Provide structure. Children crave structure, but many parents are reluctant to lay down and enforce a set of rules. When expectations are clear, children learn which behaviors are acceptable and which aren't. You'll be less stressed and anxious if you aren't battling with your kids to keep their rooms clean, help with household chores, and do their homework.

5. Don't spoil your child. Giving into a child's every whim creates ever-expanding expectations of continued indulgence. As the saying goes, "The child who has everything appreciates nothing." Saying no may be painful in the short run, but it leads to fewer anxiety-inducing temper tantrums (and other negative behaviors) in the medium and long run.

6. Manage your child's technology. If you're addicted to technology, your kids likely will be, too. There's a lot of nasty stuff on the Web, including bullying through social media. Instead of worrying about it, put filters and time limits on computer and cell phone usage. If you buy a cell phone for your child, specify that you have the right to look at it any time you want.

7. Let teenagers be teenagers. Yes, they'll likely be moody and uncommunicative sometimes. Leave the lines of communication open, and ride the waves of their raging hormones. Have frank conversations about sex, dating, and safety. Your kids will appreciate it, and they'll be less likely to lie about their activities and friendships.

8. Don't fight your kids' dating choices. Just as you dated plenty of people whom your parents didn't like, so too will your children bring home boyfriends/girlfriends that aren't good-looking enough, ambitious enough, or smart enough. You'll be a much calmer person if you let these relationships run their course. Most of them won't work out, and then you can breathe a gentle sigh of relief. If you *do* like the current boyfriend or girlfriend, don't become too emotionally involved with them. A lot of unpleasant family dynamics can occur when a relationship breaks up and the parents stay in touch with the ex.

9. Don't enable a dependent lifestyle. So … your child has graduated from college and has moved back home, where you cook his meals and do his laundry while collecting exactly $0 room and board. It's one thing to help your children get on their feet and establish themselves as adults; it's another to enable a dependent lifestyle in which they have no motivation to work, pay their bills, or live independently. Dependent adult children will always be a source of stress and anxiety for you, so nip dependency in the bud. Set a timeline for moving out or cutting off of financial support. "But she can't afford an apartment!" you will worry. But, when the only other option is homelessness, she'll figure something out. If she doesn't like sharing a house with nine housemates, she'll be motivated to find a better job, make more money, and split expenses with one roommate instead of nine.

10. If your kids are adults, butt out. Many parents say they want a close relationship with their adult children, when what they really want is control. After your kids have moved out of your home and established their own lives, they get to do what they want, whether you like it or not. Keep your opinions to yourself, don't interfere in their relationships, and smile a lot (especially if you want to see your grandchildren).

73. Take (Some of) the Worry Out of Travel

Some of us love travel, with its head mixture of exotic settings, rich history, and potential romance. For others, travel is nothing but a series of missed connections, lost luggage, sleazy hotel rooms, and sleepless nights.

If you're a homebody who doesn't like to travel but needs to do so for business, family, or other reasons, here are some suggestions for keeping your travel anxiety under control.

1. Plan, plan, plan. The more aspects of your trip that you can plan and choose, the greater your sense of control—and the lower your anxiety. For example, you can find reviews of just about all accommodations on the Web. Guests often post candid photos that may differ greatly from the glossy, shiny photos on the motel or B&B's website.

2. Choose your seat early and carefully. If you're traveling via bus, train, or airplane, make your reservation far enough in advance that you get to choose the seat that you want. Need to use the bathroom regularly? Choose an aisle seat. Like the view? Choose a window seat. Wait too long to make a reservation, and you'll end up with that dreaded middle seat.

3. Claim the overhead compartment. Many air travelers worry themselves sick about the overhead bins having enough room to hold their carry-on language. Check out the airline's seating policy and choose a seat that ensures early boarding—and the likelihood of available overhead space.

4. Bring along the comforts of home. Make your accommodations more comfortable by making them more familiar. If you like to fall asleep to the sounds of a white noise machine, bring it with you. You can also pack a favorite pillow, blanket, or bathrobe.

5. Arrive early. Almost nothing is more stressful about air travel than the fear of missing a flight. Arrive at the airport two hours before the flight is scheduled to depart, which should give you enough time to check in, get through security, and find the gate.

6. Keep yourself occupied. If you're driving a long distance, make sure you have podcasts, books on tape, and music downloaded and ready to help you pass the time. If you're not behind the wheel, bring your computer, cell phone, or tablet and play video games or watch movies. Also pack books and magazines to give your eyes a break from staring at a screen.

7. Breathe. For many air travelers, the most stressful parts of the flight are takeoff and landing. To prevent yourself from hyperventilating, use the square breathing technique explained in Tip #56.

8. Pack 24 hours in advance. Packing on the day of your trip will only add more stress to a day that's already jam-packed. Plan to finish your packing a full 24 hours before you start the first leg of your journey. If you travel regularly, keep a list of "must-have" items in your luggage, and use it as a checklist as you do your packing. (P.S.: Whenever possible, travel light. Do you really need 10 pairs of pants and 8 shirts?)

9. Prepare yourself for bumps in the road. Your travel anxiety is probably based on experience. You know something is likely to go wrong; you just don't know what that problem will be. The solution: Prepare yourself for the most common mishaps. Pack toiletries and a change of underwear in your carry-on so that you're not caught totally off guard by lost luggage. Purchase travel insurance in case something comes up and you can't make the flight. Check out the flight route: If your flight connects through Minneapolis in January, look for a different flight that connects through a city that is less likely to be snowed in. If you think there's a chance that you'll miss your connection (it happens all the time), book a hotel room in the connecting city in advance. You may have to pay a cancellation fee, but the peace of mind will be worth it. Screaming babies are common; have a set of ear buds ready so that your favorite music can drown out the caterwauling.

10. Grin and bear it. Unless you're wealthy enough to own a private jet or to fly first class, you can be pretty sure that the experience of traveling from here to there will be uncomfortable at best to downright miserable at worst. Let your mantra be: "This will all be over soon." Know that your seat will be cramped and the food will be bad and overpriced: "This will all be over soon." Some of your fellow passengers will be rude, self-centered, or obnoxious: "This will all be over soon." You miss your connection and sit in an airport for eight hours waiting for the next flight: "This will all be over soon."

74. Cope with Social Anxiety

Afraid to look like foolish in public? Worried that others won't like you? Fearful that people will reject you? Terrified of being the center of attention and certain that you'll embarrass yourself?

If the thought of interacting with others socially makes you sweat or feel nauseated, you probably experience social anxiety, an extremely common condition that affects approximately 15 million American adults.

Licensed therapists can treat severe cases of social anxiety disorder quite effectively. If you suffer from only mild or moderate social anxiety, here are some suggestions.

1. Be selective about the invitations you accept. If you avoid all social situations, you may find it difficult to meet new people, make new friends, or network your skills and business. But you can choose which parties and events you really need to attend and which you don't. Think in terms of a scorecard: What are the benefits of attending? Do they outweigh the discomfort I'll feel?

2. Use the buddy system. A supportive friend, family member, or co-worker can be a lifesaver in social situations. It's much easier to walk into a roomful of 100 people when you know and like at least one of them.

3. Set a time limit. Some people are natural partygoers; they'll be the first to arrive and the last to leave. That's not you, so don't "should" all over yourself. Determine how much time you'll stay at the gathering, and then stick to your plan. An "appearance" can require as little as thirty minutes.

4. Learn the art of small talk. At many gatherings, you'll meet a bunch of people whom you'll never see again. Rather than having an hour-long conversation with a close friend, you'll be having 12 five-minute conversations with strangers. Ask people to tell you about their children or grandchildren, and those five minutes will fly by. Talking about the weather can fill in any uncomfortable gaps. No political discussions, please.

5. Extend a hand. If you scan the room, you're likely to see others who seem ill at ease. Introduce yourself and have a chat. They'll be happy to have someone to talk with, and you'll have occupied five or ten minutes of your required party time.

6. Challenge your self-defeating or negative thought processes. For more information, see Tips #17, 43, and 53.

7. Begin with a compliment. Nothing breaks the ice like a compliment, so start conversations with a statement that will grab the person's attention: "I love your dress," "Your wedding ring is so unique," "I heard you're a great coach." Then let the person speak while you listen and nod.

8. Keep the conversation flowing. The surest conversation killers are one-word answers. If someone asks you a question, answer it and then ask a question in return. Keep it light: "Oh, I live in Cincinnati. Where do you live?" "I'm an accountant, what do you do?"

9. Set goals. You may not enjoy social gatherings, but you can get through them by viewing them as life tasks that must be accomplished. Set goals for the gathering, such as "Meet so-and-so, who's the president of such-and-such" or "Ask for advice about good local plumbers and electricians."

10. Have a panic release valve. If your anxiety starts to overwhelm you and you feel the need to flee, retreat for a couple of minutes instead of disappearing without a trace. Use the restroom, even if you don't need to. Pretend that you need to retrieve something from your car. Gaze with rapt attention at a painting or other piece of art. Breathe deeply and return to the gathering. Always greet the host upon arriving, and thank him or her as you leave.

75. Deal with Family-Based Anxieties

Many of us want to be part of a big, happy, loving family, but very few real families resemble those in feature-length Disney films. If your family members—either close or distant—tend to add to your anxieties, consider the following suggestions.

1. Say "No" to requests for money. It happens to everyone sooner or later: A family member calls or shows up and asks for a "loan." Here's the one response that works every time: "I'd like to help, but I just don't have it." If you get pushback ("But you live in a nice house," "But you make plenty of money"), the following response should end the conversation: "The problem is, I'm in debt up to my eyeballs and I'm not even sure I can afford the car payment/mortgage payment/utility bill this month."

2. Don't gossip. Your words as a gossiper will almost certainly get back to the gossipee. Do you need that drama? You do not. Smile and nod.

3. Remember: The less they know, the louder they talk. Keep this truism in mind when an obnoxious relative is braying even more aggressively than usual.

4. Don't give advice unless someone asks for it. Most likely, the person is looking to talk about his or her situation and already knows how s/he's going to respond to it. Listen, nod, and make occasional sounds of commiseration.

5. Indulge elderly relatives. They've earned it.

6. Reminisce. You may have grown apart from your siblings and cousins, but you all have one thing in common: the past. Talking about the old days can pass the time in a way that makes everyone smile. Focus on happy memories rather than tragic events.

7. Bite your tongue. Do you really need to make that snappy comeback or lob that veiled criticism over the net? De-escalate.

8. Respond to criticism with cheerfulness. Doing so instantly deflates your critic.

> *Critic:* I see you're still wearing those same old shoes.
>
> *You:* I know, aren't they awful? But they're so comfortable.
>
> *Critic:* Ummm…

> *Critic:* Your child's really rude/out of control/lazy/useless.
>
> *You:* Oh, that's an understatement. I'm dropping him off at the orphanage on the way home.
>
> *Critic:* Ummm …

9. Don't get in the middle. Cousin A may ask you to intervene in a dispute he's having with Cousin B. Nothing good can result from your involvement. Your standard response: "This is something you two have to work out between you."

10. Appreciate. Family may drive you crazy, but they've been there for you in the past, and many of them would bail you out of prison if they had to. Be thankful and overlook the small annoyances and offenses. Most likely, you aren't perfect, either.

76. Lessen Your Fears About Your Health

I've had this throbbing pain in my leg for a couple of weeks … Is amputation just around the corner? My stomach hurts … Do I have a tumor the size of a grapefruit? I feel tired by late afternoon … Am I developing narcolepsy?

We all suffer from occasional mysterious ailments that disappear as mysteriously as they appeared, but for people who live with anxiety, such ailments can seem like the first step on a quick march to the grave. The following tips may help you worry less about your health.

1. Don't Google your way to misery. Looking up your symptoms on the Web can be a prescription for panic. All roads seem to lead to cancer or death. You can find decent background information on MayoClinic.org or WebMD.com. After that, let a doctor—not the Internet—diagnose you.

2. Lose weight. Many health issues can be solved through weight loss. For example, people who are flirting with Type 2 Diabetes can often solve that problem by dropping 10% of their body weight. Exercise (see Tip #19) not only helps you lose weight but also keeps your anxiety under control.

3. Consider your age. As you get older, your body will start to behave in ways that you never expected. Maybe you have to get up to pee in the middle of the night, or you bruise more easily. Rather than fight the inevitable, accept it as a part of aging and manage the symptoms according to your doctor's advice.

4. Accommodate. Many bodily issues are benign and nothing to worry about, so don't use your emotional energy worrying about them. For example, some people develop an occasional slight shakiness, called essential tremor, in their hands. Their minds jump straight to Parkinson's Disease, but essential tremor is easily lived with. See your doctor for a diagnosis—the sooner, the better.

5. Don't fight medication. A lot of criticism has been leveled at so-called "Western medicine," with its emphasis on prescription drugs. The truth is that medications have helped tens of millions of people recover from illnesses and live longer, healthier, happier lives. If your doctor prescribes medication, it's because you need it. Fill the prescription and take it as directed.

6. Don't let your thoughts spiral out of control. If you have a tendency to go directly to the worst-case scenario, catch yourself as you begin the downward spiral. (See Tip #65.) Distract yourself by doing something that engages your full attention.

7. Ensure that your children are cared for. Many people who worry about their health fear that their children will end up abused, neglected, or poor. Alleviate that worry by putting guardianship plans in place.

8. Maintain yourself. Schedule semiannual physicals, which can detect potential problems early. Do as the doctor recommends: Quit smoking, decrease your salt intake, walk 30 minutes a day, and so on. When the doctor says something is "not a big deal" or "nothing to worry about," then it is not a big deal, and you should not worry about it.

9. Prevent obsessive self-checking. Constantly checking on a part of your body that you find worrisome (say, a toenail or a skin tag) can keep you caught in a vortex of ever-heightening worry. The more you look, or the more you pick at a part of your body, the more likely you are to develop a problem that you didn't already have. Distract yourself and breathe.

10. Talk to a therapist. Cognitive behavioral therapy (see Tip #99) can be very useful in treating excessive anxiety about your health.

77. Worry Less About Your Job

Job worries are often closely related to money worries: No job means no income. Employment in the twenty-first century has become precarious, and many people fear that they'll find themselves suddenly unemployed and unable to find another decent-paying job.

You can't control what happens at your place of business, but you can take steps to decrease your anxiety about your job and job-related matters.

1. Continue your education. You may see the writing on the wall: Your industry is contracting and your company has gone through several rounds of layoffs. Now is the time to go back to school, to get certified in a skill that's in demand. Yes, it will take time—usually at least a year or two. But you'll have something to fall back on.

2. Contribute to, and don't touch, a nest egg. You should have at least a full year's worth of expenses saved. That way, if you become unemployed, you can devote all your time to the job search and none of your time to worrying about the bills.

3. Moonlight. Take extra jobs on the evenings and weekends (so long as your terms of employment don't prevent you from doing so). You'll be earning extra money while developing a client base.

4. Nod, smile, and stay quiet. No matter what your boss says, s/he does not want your opinion. S/he wants you to do what you're told. Remain quiet (but not surly) in meetings, take notes, and do what you've promised to do.

5. Stay clear of malcontents. In every workplace you'll find coworkers who love nothing more than stirring the pot, complaining about anything and everything. They'll suck you into their vortex of misery, so refrain from engaging with them while remaining polite and collegial.

6. Avoid office politics. If you're the type of person who wants to hold a good job and not rule the company or the world, don't get mixed up in office politics, which are extremely stressful and anxiety inducing. If you do want to rule the world, then you're the type of person who's creating the worries that readers of this book are trying to manage.

7. Pretend to care. Every company wants its employees 100% "with the program," but your company doesn't own you. Even if you think the latest initiative is the stupidest idea you've ever heard, get with it enthusiastically even if you couldn't care less. There will be some cost to your soul, but the trade-off is worth it.

8. Develop your professional network. Most people find jobs through friends and colleagues, so keep your contacts list updated. LinkedIn is a great place to build a network. It's free and easy to use, so sign up today.

9. Remember: Loyalty is no more. The days of company loyalty to employees are over. Do a good job, but remember that your loyalty should be to yourself. If a better opportunity comes your way: Take it. Your status as a favored employee can disintegrate overnight with a change in management or ownership.

10. Spend time with friends and family. Nothing reduces anxiety better than laughing and enjoying social time with people you like and love. Socializing is even more important when you have a stressful job, so schedule get-togethers just as you'd schedule meetings and presentations. Any time away from the worries of the workplace is time well spent.

78. If You're Single—Manage Your Dating Anxiety

Single people of all ages spend an enormous amount of their personal time in the quest for a mate. Dating apps have created a nationwide, even worldwide, marketplace for potential partners. In some ways, there's almost too much variety: When you think you may have found the right person, you may hear a little voice whispering in your ear, "But there may be someone even better just around the next corner."

There's no doubt that dating can be stressful. Here are some tips to reduce your dating anxieties.

1. Remember: You're right for someone. Many people fear that they'll never meet their life partner. Understand that there's someone out there who will find you wildly appealing. Finding that person may take plenty of time and effort, but it *will* happen.

2. Don't ghost. If you're not interested in someone after a few dates, drop that person a note in which you say politely but unequivocally that you no longer want to pursue the relationship. "I've decided to get back with my ex" is a little white lie that extricates you while not hurting the other person's feelings. You'll sleep better knowing you did the right thing.

3. If you're ghosted, don't freak out. Ghosting happens every day; it will likely happen to you sooner or later. If and when it does happen, accept it and let it go, even if you really liked the other person. Why would you want to be with somebody who engages in such behavior?

4. Meet quickly. If you're meeting people through a dating app, a quick phone call (maximum 15 minutes) should be enough to establish interest. Don't spend weeks or months texting, emailing, and calling before you meet. Doing so only raises expectations and anxiety levels as you worry, "When are we finally going to meet?" There's no substitute for in-person chemistry.

5. Make no commitments until you are ready to do so, and don't ask for commitments until a suitable amount of time has passed. It is perfectly acceptable to date several people simultaneously, as long as you spell out your approach to dating upfront. Beware of anyone who wants an insta-relationship.

6. Don't ignore red flags. Physical attraction can cause us to discount major warning signals about the other person. Pay attention to, and closely monitor, possibly concerning behaviors or attitudes. Cut bait when you need to.

7. Don't obsess over another person. Anxiety-prone people can get caught in a thought loop: Why hasn't he called me? Why hasn't she responded to my text? Why did he say he's not available this weekend? Why does she seem more interested in her cell phone than in me? Negative thought loops are the bête noir of people with anxiety. Take it one step at a time. If the other person isn't responding when you reach out, then remember the classic line from *Sex in the City:* "He's [or she's] just not that into you." Move on.

8. Show your true self. Many (but certainly not all) people are on their best behavior on the first few dates. After that, it's time to let your hair down. At some point, your romantic partner has to see you without make-up or notice your bald spot and paunch. Attempting to maintain a façade is extremely wearying and anxiety inducing. After the first few dates, it's time to be who you are and let the relationship run its course.

9. Post a realistic photo of yourself. Set a good example for the singles of the world and post a recent, realistic photo of yourself on your dating profile. All the filters and Photoshop in the world aren't going to change your appearance when you meet in person.

10. Remember: Dating should be fun. If it produces too much stress or anxiety, you're probably dating the wrong people. Be practical, know what you want, separate the wheat from the chaff, and find the person who brings out the best in you instead of your anxious self.

79. Control Anxiety Around the Holidays

For many people, the holidays (particularly the Christmas-Chanukah-Kwanzaa-New Year's nexus) are extremely stressful. Instead of enjoying well-deserved time off work, they worry about gift-giving, hosting, family politics, and a million other details that turn the holidays into an ordeal.

If the holidays trigger your anxiety, try the following.

1. Don't aim for, or expect, perfection. Nobody expects your home, your meal, your hors d'oeuvres, or your decorations to be perfect. Neither should you.

2. Don't overindulge in alcohol. You might be tempted to drink more than usual to get through the holidays. An occasional drink is fine, but don't overdo it. (See Tip #62.)

3. Adopt a healthy approach to giving and receiving gifts. Don't go into debt to buy holidays gifts, and don't expect extravagant presents. Focus on family, friends, relationships, and gratitude. Set a spending budget and stick to it.

4. Maintain a reasonable schedule. Don't attempt to do so much that you spend all your time rushing around and little time enjoying your activities. You may need to turn down some invitations. Do so with regret, explaining your reasons, and then return the invitation during less frantic times.

5. Have some quiet time. Too much togetherness can be stressful. If you're traveling to visit relatives, rent a hotel room so that you have your own space at the end of the day. If you're staying with a friend or relative, find a reason to leave the house for an hour or two each day. Your host will appreciate it as much as you do.

6. Don't talk politics. Focus instead on happy memories, plans for the new year, and party games that make everyone laugh.

7. Start a new custom. Holidays are the perfect time for nostalgia, but they're also a great time to try something new.

8. Hire help. If you can't do it all yourself—and most likely you can't—then enlist or hire help so that you can focus on what you want to do. If money is tight, you can work on a barter system with a friend: "You help me do this now, and I'll help you do that later."

9. Maintain your daily routine. If you walk, run, or otherwise exercise, don't give it up because you're preparing for the holidays. Also maintain the same sleep schedule.

10. Accept, forgive, move on. Many families expect a full house on holidays, which can be a problem for married couples, especially when one spouse's family lives in Florida and the other spouse's family lives in Oregon. Accept that others are balancing their lives, just as you are. Don't get angry. The greatest gift you can give to children who are

planning to spend a holiday with their in-laws is your blessing.

80. Make Peace with Public Speaking

Some people love being at the front of a room, but many others dread and even fear public speaking. The odds are good, though, that at some point in your life you'll need to address a group. Rather than toss and turn as public-speaking anxiety keeps you awake, try the following suggestions for embracing the public speaker in you.

1. Acknowledge your fears. Just as acknowledging your anxieties is the first step to overcoming them (see Tip #1), owning your fears of public speaking is the first step in delivering an effective talk or presentation.

2. Know your audience. If you're presenting to a fairly small group, it will be relatively easy to learn about the individuals who will be in attendance. For larger groups, research their interests and beliefs. It's much easier to speak to a group if you feel that you already know them.

3. Practice your presentation in front of mirror. The key to effective delivery is practice, practice, practice. Record yourself, watch the video or listen to the recording, and tweak your words and mannerisms as necessary.

4. Ask for feedback. After you've practiced, do a run-through of your presentation with a sympathetic person. Ask how you can improve it. Do you need to add information? Speak less about a particular topic? Offer more interesting visual aids?

5. Open with a story. Human beings seem genetically disposed to being interested in stories. You can grab your audience's attention by starting with a brief story to bridge the gap between you and them. Don't start with a joke. Humor is subjective, and you may unintentionally give offense.

6. Appear confident, even if you are terrified. Just as smiling makes you feel happy even when you aren't, presenting a confident exterior can make you feel more confident. Talking a walk before you arrive can help to dispel some of your nervous energy.

7. Practice positive self-talk. Tell yourself that your presentation will be successful. Avoid the negative self-talk that perpetuates anxiety (see Tip #43).

8. Wear comfortable, simple, elegant clothes. You'll be able to deliver your presentation much more smoothly if your shoes aren't pinching your feet and your tie isn't too tight around your neck.

9. Breathe during your presentation. Most presenters occasionally ask the audience to participate or to contribute questions. While others are speaking, take the time to breathe deeply and to relax yourself.

10. Reward yourself. Promise yourself a reward for a well-delivered presentation, and then accept that gift from yourself.

Part III: Sleep Tips for the Anxious

Because sleeping can be difficult for those who suffer with anxiety, the last part of this book offers tips for helping you get to sleep and stay asleep. As we get started, though, be sure to manage your expectations. Can you expect that, from here on out, you will always fall asleep the second your head hits the pillow, you will always sleep soundly through the night without waking up once, and you will always wake up refreshed and renewed when the alarm goes off? No. Can you learn to fall asleep more quickly and sleep through most of the night? Yes.

81. Occasional Insomnia Is Completely Normal

Everyone has trouble falling asleep occasionally and waking up earlier than they want to. Sometimes their eyes pop open in the middle of the night and they wonder if they'll ever fall back asleep. (Usually, they do, but sometimes they don't.)

Although delayed or interrupted sleep is perfectly normal, those with anxiety may find themselves escalating occasional insomnia into a full-blown crisis. The result can be sleep anxiety, which occurs when your concerns about falling asleep turn into a worrisome ordeal. Rather than preparing your body for a night's rest, you worry: Will I lie there, wide awake, all night long? Will I toss and turn? Will I be exhausted all day tomorrow? Your negative thought loop becomes a self-fulfilling prophecy, and your sleep anxiety keeps you awake. At the same time, your bed becomes a place of torment rather than a venue for restful slumber.

So take a moment to say to yourself: I'll fall asleep. Once in a while, I'll wake up in the middle of the night. It's OK. It happens. If my sleep is poor for a few nights in a row, my body will be so tired that I'm guaranteed a good night's sleep a few days from now. And a few days will pass in the blink of an eye.

82. If You Get Up to Pee, You'll Have No Trouble Falling Asleep Again

Many people, especially people of a certain age, feel a pressing on their bladder that wakes them up before the alarm clock rings. They resist going to the bathroom to relieve their bladder because they believe that doing so will wake their body and that they won't fall sleep again when they return to bed.

That belief is completely false. In fact, staying in bed when you have to pee prevents you from sleeping soundly. Your body is saying to you, "Pee now," and you're fighting it. You'll never sleep well unless you empty your bladder. So stumble to the bathroom, urinate, and then crawl back into your comfy bed, secure in the knowledge that you'll be asleep almost instantly.

83. Detach Yourself from All Screens Two Hours Before Bed

The blue light emitted by your television, tablet, cell phone, and other electronic technologies is the enemy of sleep. This light tricks your body into believing it's daytime, when the human body is programmed to be active and awake, not asleep. It also inhibits your body's natural production of melatonin, a hormone that signals your body that it's time to sleep.

Make a promise to yourself: You will separate yourself from all screens, totally and completely, for the two hours before you turn in. By doing so, you'll allow your body's natural desire to sleep to take hold. It won't have to compete with YouTube videos, Facebook updates, dramatic Tweets, and the other electronic beeps and blips that demand your attention when you should be shutting down your attention for the night.

If you tend to work late into the night, you can add a blue-light filter to your technology. Many blue-light-reducing programs and apps are available, including Bluelight Filter, Easy Eyes, f.lux, Night Owl, and Nightshift. You can also wear amber-tinted glasses if you like to watch television at night.

84. Use Your Bedroom Only for Sleep and Sex

Many people have turned their bedroom into a multimedia recreation room. By doing so, they signal to their minds that the room is to be used for many different activities. In other words, the mind doesn't see the bedroom and think "Ah, sleep." It thinks, "Oh, so many possibilities."

If you live in a large enough space, use your bedroom only for sleep and sex (both done in bed). In other words, train yourself to think of your bedroom as your sleep sanctuary, the place where you reward yourself by sleeping off the stresses of the day or having sex with your partner (and then falling asleep afterward).

If your living space is relatively small, such as a studio apartment, you can cordon off your sleep space with a screen or a curtain. Consider the creation of your room-within-a room a design challenge: How can you separate your bed from the rest of the unit in an aesthetically pleasing way that beckons you and welcomes you for a great night's sleep?

85. Keep All Your Technology in Another Room

You may be so attached to your technology—especially your cell phone—that you can't imaging not having it within arm's reach at any given moment. By keeping your phone on your nightstand, or even in bed with you, you are giving the world permission to interrupt your sleep. Instead of insisting, "My bed is my special place, where I slumber like an angel," you say, "Friends, family, social media: I'm available whenever you want me. You're more important to me than my sleep is."

So: Leave your tablet, your laptop, your phone in another room, and before you do so—silence them or turn them off. The only sounds that should be allowed to waken you are your pleasant alarm clock (see Tip #46), the chirping of birds, or the comforting drizzle of rain.

86. Monitor Your Exercise Schedule

Using exercise to keep your body and mind occupied, and to manage your anxiety, is highly effective (see Tip #19). However, be mindful of your workout schedule. Working out too soon before bedtime stimulates your body to produce adrenaline, which may prevent you from falling asleep.

If you think that a nighttime exercise schedule is interfering with your ZZZ's, try to work out earlier in the day. Morning or afternoon workouts are generally best, but if your work schedule prevents exercise during the daytime, try to work out as early in the evening as possible, perhaps on your way home from work.

And take heart in the knowledge that, in general, exercising at any time of day helps you sleep better that night.

87. Ensure That Your Bedroom Is Quiet, Dark, and Cool

The physical characteristics of your sleeping space can either help or hinder your ability to fall asleep and stay asleep.

First, ensure that your bedroom is as quiet as you can make it. If you live in a busy neighborhood or city, invest in a white-noise machine to cover up annoying noises such as trucks backing up or ambulances racing down the avenue. If you tend to fall asleep with the television on, set the TV to turn itself off.

Second, make your sleep space as close to pitch-black as you can. Light signals the body to wake up, so keep your room dark as night. Buy room-darkening shades; they're extremely effective. Don't go to bed with an illuminated night light in the room. Close your door to seal out sound and light from other areas of the house or apartment.

Third, before bed turn down the thermostat to a maximum of 65 degrees. A cool room is essential to falling and staying asleep. If you tend to sleep cold, pile on cozy comforters and blankets rather than turn up the heat.

88. Slow Your Racing Thoughts

Many who suffer from anxiety manage the symptoms by keeping themselves busy, and their brains occupied, throughout the day. Then, when it's time to lie down and fall asleep, all the anxieties they've tamped down during the day come back with a vengeance. Their minds start racing, and they can't seem to switch off their brain and allow sleep to take over.

Try a few easy techniques to prevent your brain from running amok when you're trying to get unconscious:

- Count sheep. In this time-honored technique, you force yourself to stop thinking about your worries and instead slowly count backwards from 100. If your worries interfere, start again at 100.
- Use "Don't Think" as a mantra. Slowly repeat the phrase "Don't think" over and over in your mind. Worrisome thoughts may invade; just push them aside and keep thinking, "Don't think."
- Envision a blank sheet of white paper. To clear your mind, picture a sheet of unlined white paper of the kind you might use in your printer. Each time your mind wanders, bring it back to the sheet of white paper.

You might also try a sleep app, such as Aura: Calm Anxiety & Sleep, Pzizz, Relax & Sleep Well, Relax Melodies, or Sleep Cycle. Experiment to see which one works best for you.

89. Get Out of Bed After 15 Sleepless Minutes

This one may be tough, but it works.

If you've gone to bed, but you're still tossing and turning after 15 minutes, get out of bed, go to another room, and spend 15 minutes reading a printed book or magazine—*not* perusing an article on a computer screen, and *not* watching a video on your tablet. Your body is telling you it's not ready for sleep yet, so don't frustrate yourself (and possibly increase your sleep anxiety—see Tip #98) by trying to force yourself into sleep. Reading is the perfect way to move your body and mind from a state of wakefulness to a state of sleep preparedness. When you start to feel sleepy, return to bed, and if you're still tossing and turning, get up and read for another 15 minutes. Repeat as often as necessary until you're sleeping like a baby.

90. Be Careful What You Eat and Drink Before Bed

Late-night snacking isn't good for your waistline, and it can interfere with your sleep, too, because your body can't relax fully while it's working to digest a lot of food. Some people find a (very) small snack before bed to be helpful; the key here is the smallness of the snack. Don't load up on sugar or caffeine before bed, and limit caffeine intake during the day (see Tip #26). One study showed that drinking caffeine as much as six hours before bed can seriously disrupt your sleep.

In addition, drinking alcohol won't improve your sleep. It may help you fall asleep more quickly, but as the body metabolizes the alcohol, it will turn to sugar, flooding your bloodstream, stimulating you, and waking you up.

Even drinking healthy fluids such as water before bed may interfere with sleep by causing your bladder to feel full as you're getting into bed. Try to use the bathroom before turning in for the night to reduce the odds of nighttime awakenings.

Some studies have shown that drinking a few ounces of tart cherry juice before bed can help with insomnia.

91. Try a Change of Venue

You've been busy all day, taking care of business and putting out fires. You throw yourself into bed, expecting to sleep like a baby because you've earned it. And then it happens. As you lie in your dark bedroom in a state of sensory deprivation, all your anxieties can come charging forward. You can't find a comfortable position, the sheets feel scratchy, and there's an annoying lump in your pillow that won't go away no matter how many times you punch it.

A change of sleep venue may be helpful here. Get out of bed, take your blanket with you, and move onto the couch, a bed in the spare bedroom, or a futon in the basement. By changing your venue, you've changed the environment that was preventing you from falling asleep. When you rid yourself of the sleep anxiety associated with your bed and bedroom (see Tip #81), you may find yourself falling asleep quickly in the new location.

92. Drink Warm Milk

When you were a child, your mother may have given you a cup of warm milk to help you sleep on a restless night. If it worked when you were a child, then it may work when you are an adult.

While there is little scientific evidence to suggest that the physical components of (natural compounds in) milk will induce sleep, the mere association between drinking warm milk and sleeping may help lull you into a state of blissful drowsiness. In other words, if you believe that a comforting cup of warm milk helps you fall asleep, then it may very well do so.

Hardcore lab science may not have proven that drinking warm milk is the equivalent of a sleeping pill, but it has proven the powerful mind-body connection. If you think it works, then it probably will.

93. Set and Maintain a Sleep Schedule

Like all animals, human beings have natural body rhythms that are tied to the 24-hour cycle of the day. Put simply, our bodies want to be awake during the day and asleep at night. Electric light—which allows us to stay awake long past our natural bedtime—has been available for only a tiny fraction of human history. Our ancestors had to farm, hunt, and gather during the daylight, and they needed a safe space to hunker down and sleep at night, when the only source of natural light was the moon.

Work with your body's natural rhythms by creating and sticking to a sleep schedule. Go to bed at the same time every night, and wake up at the same time every day. Doing so can help your body create a routine in which it *expects* to sleep, which can make it easier to fall and stay asleep.

Of course, you aren't a machine, and you may want to sleep in a bit on the weekends. An extra half hour or hour of slumber shouldn't knock off your rhythm, so go ahead and enjoy that extra time in bed—just don't read the newspaper there, as your bedroom should reserved exclusively for sleep and sex (see Tip #84).

94. Avoid Conflict in the Evening

It's not easy to schedule the conflict in our lives. It can flare up at any minute, from the moment we wake up (maybe we've awakened to the sound of the kids pummeling each other in another room) to the minute we're ready to turn in for the night (perhaps we made the mistake of checking our email before bed, and there's an angry message from a friend or colleague).

It's unreasonable to think that you'll always be able to control the timing of your conflict, but you can take steps to avoid the interactions that will work you up into a state of agitation before bed. Have difficult conversations with co-workers during the day, and then leave those worries at work (see Tip #63). If you need to talk with your romantic partner about an issue that is likely to stir up anger, resentment, worry, or any other negative emotion, broach the subject in a neutral location—preferably not in your home, and certainly not in your bedroom—long, long before you go to bed. Doing so will give you several hours of processing time before bedtime, and you'll be less likely to toss and turn as you repeat the conversation in your head endlessly.

Today, social media are a source of endless, escalating conflict in many people's lives. If you're unwilling to give up all your social media accounts (see Tip #8), first ask yourself if you're addicted. Then make a pact with yourself that you won't check any of those accounts within three hours of bedtime.

95. Have a Conversation with Your Sleep Partner

A common (and kind) dating strategy is to end the relationship by saying, "It's not you—it's me."

At nighttime, though, it may not be you who is preventing you from sleeping. There, your partner may be at fault. Perhaps he snores and snorts. Maybe she's a blanket hog. You like the air conditioner blasting; your partner gets up and turns it off. There are as many different sleep scenarios as there are romantic couples.

If your partner is preventing you from falling asleep or waking you up, it's a good idea to have a gentle but serious conversation about it. Simple solutions and treatments are available for common sleep problems, such as snoring; sometimes it's just a matter of adjusting position, getting a new pillow, or raising one's head. A more serious condition that leads to snoring is sleep apnea, in which case medical treatment is an urgent necessity.

Romantic notions hold that loving couples must sleep together, but a couple can be very much in love while sleeping in separate beds. If you and your partner aren't sleep-compatible, separate bedrooms may be the solution.

In addition, many couples find that their sleep improves greatly when they trade up to a king-sized bed, which allows each person to have his or her own comfy blankets (instead of a shared comforter) and space, which can be particularly wonderful for people who sleep hot and don't want their partner's body heat making them uncomfortable during the night.

96. Try Melatonin and Other Natural Supplements

Melatonin is a hormone that the body produces naturally. It regulates the sleep-wake cycle, signaling your body that it's nighttime and time to relax so that you can fall asleep. For most people, melatonin levels rise about two hours before bedtime. To help your body produce melatonin at night, get exposure to natural light during the daytime. Raise those blinds and let the sun shine in; or, if you work in a dark cubbyhole or cubicle, try a light therapy box (see Tip #67).

You don't need to visit a health-food store or vitamin shop to buy melatonin. It's available just about everywhere, from the local drugstore to the big-box retailers such as Walmart and Target. If you do decide to try it, start with a small dose, 1 to 3 milligrams, two hours before bedtime. Large doses (such as 10 mg) are often overkill.

Other supplements that help some people fall sleep, stay sleep, or sleep longer include 5-HTP, gingko biloba, glycine, L-theanine, magnesium, tryptophan, and valerian root. Many supplements are sold in combinations, so you may need to experiment to find the best solution for you.

Of course, talk with your doctor before you begin taking any supplement, and monitor the effects and side effects. Stop taking any supplement that makes you feel nauseated or groggy.

97. Experiment with CBD Oil

Relatively new to the market in some states is cannabidiol (CBD) oil, which is extracted from the buds and flowers of hemp and marijuana plants. It does not produce intoxication, but many people who struggle with sleep have noted its relaxing effects.

Some scientific studies have confirmed that CBD can help with occasional insomnia (and anxiety). Shortly before bed, you simply hold a few drops under your tongue ("in suspension") for 30 to 90 seconds and then swallow the oil, which can have the pleasant taste of cinnamon, orange, vanilla, mint, or berries. The general dose is 1-6 milligrams of CBD oil for every ten pounds of body weight, but—as with all supplements—you should talk with your doctor about the possible pros and cons first.

98. Talk Yourself Out of Sleep Anxiety

As we've seen, a common accompaniment to insomnia is sleep anxiety, the dread of not being able to fall asleep, or waking up in the middle of the night, or not sleeping enough hours to feel refreshed and ready for a new day. Paradoxically, the sleep anxiety is what keeps you awake as you put pressure on yourself to *just fall asleep, damn it.*

A good long-term solution is to talk yourself out of sleep-anxious thoughts as they arise, replacing them with more realistic beliefs as you engage in a conversation with yourself. Such self-talk is often a component of a larger program of cognitive behavioral therapy, or CBT (see Tip #99).

To talk yourself out your sleep anxiety, disassemble exaggerations, catastrophizing, and other types of dysfunctional thoughts by examining them critically and adjusting them to better match reality. Here are some examples:

When you think: "If I get up to pee, I'll never fall back asleep."

Think instead: "As soon as I get back to bed from the bathroom, I'll be asleep within seconds." (See Tip # 82.)

When you think: "I'm a zombie if I don't get my eight hours of sleep."

Think instead: "I can get along just fine on six hours of sleep."

When you think: "I'm not sleeping, and this is the worst thing that could happen to me."

Think instead: "I'm not sleeping tonight, but that means I'll be tired tomorrow, and I can look forward to better sleep tomorrow night."

When you think: "I'll never fall asleep in that hotel room."
Think instead: "Maybe I won't sleep well in that hotel room, but I'll make sure to request a quiet room far away from the ice machine and the elevator. Eventually I'll be so tired that I'll sleep just fine."

With a little practice, you'll start to catch your negative thinking as soon as it begins.

99. Seek Cognitive Behavioral Therapy

There is no shame in seeking psychological therapy for insomnia. One of the most popular and successful therapeutic interventions is cognitive behavioral therapy (CBT). Rather than treating you with medications, your therapist teaches you how to recognize and challenge the beliefs that affect your ability to sleep. Working with a therapist, you learn to implement good sleep hygiene practices, talk to yourself in ways that promote (rather than banish) sleep, train yourself to relax, and use other techniques to condition yourself to fall asleep and stay asleep.

If you decide to try CBT, be patient. Unlike a sleeping pill, its effects are not immediate; most CBT programs require a commitment of about 5 to 8 weeks. Your therapist may suggest strategies that seem odd, such as sleep restriction therapy (in which you stay up several hours past your bedtime, which will make you more tired and set you up for a good night's sleep the next day) and "paradoxical intention," in which you go to bed and purposely try to stay awake. The idea behind paradoxical intention is that it helps to eliminate sleep anxiety. If you worry about falling asleep, then intentionally trying to stay awake may eliminate that worry, and paradoxically you may find yourself in slumber land.

100. When All Else Fails—Talk with Your Doctor About Prescription Medication

Many common over-the-counter medications can help with occasional sleeplessness. The most popular are diphenhydramine (the active ingredient in Benadryl) and doxylamine succinate (the active ingredient in NyQuil). Antihistamines such as cetirizine (Zyrtec) can have a sedating effect, so if you're taking an antihistamine to help allergies, be sure to take your dose at night—it might give you that little extra sleep boost.

If you're suffering from chronic insomnia, a trip to the doctor is warranted. He or she may ask you to undergo a sleep study or may prescribe a highly effective sleeping pill such as solider tartarate (Ambien). Be sure to follow your doctor's guidelines, as it is easy to become dependent on sleeping pills, and you can experience rebound insomnia when you stop taking them. Consider them the last resort when you absolutely, positively must have six or more hours of uninterrupted sleep. Use them precisely as directed. Pleasant dreams!

References

Part I: The Basics

Survey data:

Bandelow, B., & Michaelis, S. (2015). Epidemiology of anxiety disorders in the 21st century. *Dialogues in Clinical Neuroscience, 17*(3), 327–335.

Tip #8: Quit All Social Media. Now.

Social media and mental health:

Hunt, M. G., Marx, M., Lipson, C., & Young, J. (2018). No more FOMO: Limiting social media decreases loneliness and depression. *Journal of Social and Clinical Psychology, 37*(10), 751-768. https://doi.org/10.1521/jscp.2018.37.10.751

Pantic, I. (2014). Online social networking and mental health. *Cyberpsychology, Behavior, and Social Networking, 17*(10), 652–657. https://doi.org/10.1089/cyber.2014.0070.

Tip #9: Enjoy a Warm, Relaxing Bath

Benefits of bathing:

Goto, Y., Hayasaka, S., Kurihara, S., Nakamura, Y. (2018). Physical and mental effects of bathing: A randomized intervention study. *Evidence Based Complementary and Alternative Medicine*. https://doi.org/10.1155/2018/9521086

Bathing and weight loss:

Faulkner, S. H., Jackson, S., Fatania, G., & Leicht, C. A. (2017). The effect of passive heating on heat shock protein 70 and interleukin-6: A possible treatment tool for metabolic diseases? *Temperature, 4*(3), 292-304. doi:10.1080/23328940.2017.1288688

Tip #10: Break the Rumination Cycle

Psychological effects of rumination:

Nolen-Hoeksema, S., Wisco, B. E., & Lyubomirsky, S. (2008). Rethinking rumination. *Perspectives on Psychological Science, 3*, 400–424.

Tip #13: Get Out—Or Move Out—of the City

Urban statistics:

Duffin, E. (2019, Sept. 20). Urbanization by continent 2019. *Statista*, based on World Bank statistics. https://www.statista.com/statistics/270860/urbanization-by-continent/

United Nations Department of Economic and Social Affairs. (2018, May 16). 68% of world population projected to live in urban areas by 2050, says UN.

https://www.un.org/development/desa/en/news/population/2018-revision-of-world-urbanization-prospects.html

Drawbacks of living in cities:

Gruebner, O., Rapp, M. A., Adli, M., Kluge, U., Galea, S., & Heinz, A. (2017). Cities and mental health. *Deutsches Arzteblatt International, 114*(8), 121–127. https://doi.org/10.3238/arztebl.2017.0121

Lederbogen, F., Kirsch, P., Haddad, L., Streit, F., Tost, H., Schuch, P., Wüst, S., Pruessner, J. C., Reitschel, M., Deuschle, M., & Myer-Lindenberg, A. (2011). City living and urban upbringing affect neural social stress processing in humans. *Nature, 474*(7352), 498–501. https://doi.org/10.1038/nature10190

Peen, J., Schoevers, R. A., Beekman, A. T., & Dekker, J. (2010). The current status of urban-rural differences in psychiatric disorders. *Acta Psychiatrica Scandinavica, 12*(1), 84-93. https://doi.org/10.1111/j.1600-0447.2009.01438.x

Tip #17: Challenge Irrational Beliefs

List of 12 irrational beliefs:

Ellis, A. (1997). A basic clinical theory of rational-emotive therapy. In A. Ellis & R. Grieger (Eds.), *Handbook of rational-emotive therapy.* New York: Springer.

Tip #23: Find Your Flow

Flow figure:

Csikszentmihalyi, M. (1990). *Flow: The psychology of optimal experience. Steps toward enhancing the quality of life.* New York: Harper Perennial. p. 74.

Csikszentmihalyi, M. (1998). *Finding flow: The psychology of engagement with everyday life.* New York: Basic Books, p. 31.

Tip #29: Experiment with Aromatherapy

Koulivand, P. H., Ghadiri, M. K., & Gorji, A. (2013, March 14). Lavender and the nervous system. *Evidence-Based Complementary and Alternative Medicine.* doi:10.1155/2013/681304

Tip #32: Put Down Your Smart Phone

Data:

Haynes, T. (2018, May 1). Dopamine, smartphones, and you: A battle for your rime. Science in the News (Harvard University Graduate School of Arts and Sciences). http://sitn.hms.harvard.edu/flash/2018/dopamine-smartphones-battle-time/

Tip #35: Make Time for Romance—But Cut Yourself Some Slack

Similarities among friends and romantic partners:

Layton, B., & Insko, C. (1974). Anticipated Interaction and the Similarity-Attraction Effect. *Sociometry, 37*(2), 149-162. doi:10.2307/2786372

Montoya, R. M., Horton, R. S., & Kirchner, J. (2008). Is actual similarity necessary for attraction? A meta-analysis of actual and perceived similarity. *Journal of Social and Personal Relationships, 25*(6), 889-922. https://doi.org/10.1177/0265407508096700

Youyou, W., Stillwell, D., Schwartz, A., & Kosinski, M. (2017). Birds of a feather do flock together: Behavior-based personality assessment method reveal personality similarity among couples and friends. *Psychological Science, 28*(3), 276-284, https://doi.org/10.1177/0956797616678187

Tip #38: Indulge in (Reasonable) Retail Therapy

Retail therapy improves mood:

Atalay, A. S., & Meloy, M. G. (2011, May 2). Retail therapy: A strategic effort to improve mood. *Psychology and Marketing.* https://doi.org/10.1002/mar.20404

Tip #43: Break the Cycle of Negative Thinking

Beck, A. T. (1976). *Cognitive therapy and the emotional disorders*. New York, NY: International Universities Press.

Beck, A. T., Rush, A. J., Shaw, B. F., & Emery, G. (1987). *Cognitive therapy of depression*. New York, NY: Guilford Press.

Clark, D. A., & Beck, A. T. (2011). *Cognitive therapy of anxiety disorders: Science and practice*. New York, NY: Guilford Press.

Tip #50. Drink Chamomile Tea

Chamomile as an anxiolytic:

Sarris, J., Panossian, A., Schweitzer, I., Stough C., & Scholey, A. (2011). Herbal medicine for depression, anxiety, and insomnia: A review of psychopharmacology and clinical evidence. *European Neuropsychopharmacology, 21*(12), 841-860.

Antiviral effects of honey:

Watanabe, W., Rahmasari, R., Matsunga, A., Haruyama, T., & Kobayashi, N. (2014). Anti-influenza viral effects of honey *in vitro:* Potent high activity of Manuka honey. *Archives of Medical Research, 45*(5), 359-365.

Tip #52: Chew Gum

Nishigawa, K., Suzuki, Y., & Matsuka, Y. (2015). Masticatory performance alters stress relief effect of gum chewing. *Journal of Prosthodontic Research, 59*(4), 262-267.

Smith, A. P., Chaplin, K., & Wadsworth, E. (2012). Chewing gum, occupational stress, work performance, and well-being: An intervention study. *Appetite, 58*(3), 1083-1086.

Tip #53: Train Away Distorted Thought Patterns

Burns, D. D. (2012). *Feeling good: The new mood therapy*. New York: HarperCollins.

Leahy, R. L. (2017). *Cognitive therapy techniques: A practitioner's guide* (2nd ed.). New York, NY: Guilford Press.

Tip #54: Practice Gratitude

The phrase "Masters of the Universe" comes from Tom Wolfe's novel *The Bonfire of the Vanities* (Farrar, Straus, & Giroux, 1987).

Tip #57: Avoid Procrastination

Cutting yourself slack for procrastinating in the past:

Wohl, M., Pychyl, T., & Bennett, S. (2010). I forgive myself, now I can study: How self-forgiveness for procrastinating can reduce future procrastination. *Personality and Individual Differences, 48*(7), 803-808. doi:10.1016/j.paid.2010.01.029

Tip #58: Stand Up Straight and Tall

Chansky, T. E. (2012). *Freeing yourself from anxiety: 4 simple steps to overcome worry and create the life you want.* Boston, MA: DaCapo Lifelong Books.

Tip #60: Choose Your Colors

Kutchma, T. M. (2003). Effects of room color on stress perception: Red versus green environments, *Journal of Undergraduate Research at Minnesota State University, Mankato*, Vol. 3, Article 3. http://cornerstone.lib.mnsu.edu/jur/vol3/iss1/3

Lowe, E. Introducing: The world's most relaxing color and how to use it in your bedroom. Mindbodygreen/MBG Lifestyle. https://www.mindbodygreen.com/articles/why-navy-blue-is-officially-the-worlds-most-relaxing-color

Smith, G. F. and the University of Sussex. (2019). *The world's favorite colour: Report no. 1. A global research study investigating the psychology of colour. Conducted by Colorplan and published by G. F. Smith.* Hull and London, UK.

Tip #61: Go 21 Days Without Complaining

Table:

Bowen, W. (2007). *A complaint-free world: The 21-day challenge. How to stop complaining and start enjoying the life you always wanted.* New York, NY: Doubleday, p. 105.

Tip #62: Limit Alcohol and Quit Smoking

Corliss, J. (2020, January 29). Is red wine actually good for your heart? *Harvard Health Blog.* https://www.health.harvard.edu/blog/is-red-wine-good-actually-for-your-heart-2018021913285

Creamer, M. R., Wang, T. W., Babb, S., Cullen, K. A., Day, H., Willis, G., Jamal, A., & Neff, L. (2019). Tobacco product use and cessation indicators among Adults – United States, 2018. *Morbidity and Mortality Weekly Report 2019, 68*(45) 1013-1019.

Grant, B. F., Chou, S. P., Saha, T. D., Pickering, R. P., Kerridge, B. T., Ruan, W. J., Huang, B., Jung, J., Zhang, H., Fan, A., & Hasin, D. S. (2017). Prevalence of 12-month alcohol use, high-risk drinking, and DSM-IV Alcohol Use Disorder in the United States, 2001-2002 to 2012-2013: Results from the National Epidemiologic Survey on Alcohol and Related Conditions. *JAMA Psychiatry, 74*(9), 911-923. doi:10.1001/jamapsychiatry.2017.2161

Manthey, M., Shield, K. D., Rylett, M., Hasan, O. S. M., Probst, C., & Rehm, J. (2019). Global alcohol exposure between 1990 and 2017 and forecasts until 2030: A modelling study. *The Lancet, 393*(10190), 2493-2502.

Tip #65: Listen to the Most Relaxing Song in the World

Curtin, M. (2017, May 30). Neuroscience says listening to this song reduces anxiety by up to 65 percent. *Inc.* https://www.inc.com/melanie-curtin/neuroscience-says-listening-to-this-one-song-reduces-anxiety-by-up-to-65-percent.html

Radox Spa. (n.d.). A study investigating the effects of the music track *Weightless* by Marconi Union in consultation with Lyz Cooper. https://www.britishacademyofsoundtherapy.com/wp-content/uploads/2019/10/Mindlab-Report-Weightless-Radox-Spa.pdf

Tip #66: Develop an Internal Locus of Control

Archer, R. P. (1980). Relationships between locus of control and anxiety. *Journal of Personality Assessment, 43*(6), 617-26.

Hovenkamp Hermelink, J. H. M., Jeronimus, B. F., van der Veen, D. C., Spinhoven, P., Phennix, B. W. J. H., Schoevers, R. A., & Riese, H. (2019). Differential associations of locus of control with anxiety, depression, and life events: A five-way, nine-year study to test stability and change. *Journal of Affective Disorders, 253,* 26-34.

Tip #67: Get Enough Light Early in the Day

Use of phototherapy for anxiety:

Youngstedt, S. D., & Kripke, D. F. (2007). Does bright light have an anxiolytic effect? An open trial. *BC Psychiatry,* 7, 62. https://doi.org/10.1186/1471-244X-7-62

Tip #68: Take Your Vitamins

Vitamins A and E:

Gautam, M., Agrawal, M., Gautam, M., Sharma, P., Gautam, A. S., & Gautam, S. (2012). Role of antioxidants in generalised anxiety disorder and depression. *Indian Journal of Psychiatry, 54*(3), 244–247. doi:10.4103/0019-5545.102424

Vitamin B:

Lewis, J. E., Tiozzo, E., Melillo, A. B., Leonard, S., Chen, L., Mendez, A., Woolger, J. M., & Konefal, J. (2013). The effect of methylated vitamin B complex on depressive and anxiety symptoms and quality of life in adults with depression. *ISRN Psychiatry,* 2013:621453. https://doi.org/10.1155/2013/621453

Vitamin C:

de Oliveira, I., de Souza, V. V., Motta, V., & Da-Silva, S. L., (2015). Effects of oral Vitamin C supplementation on anxiety in students: A double-blind, randomized, placebo-controlled trial. *Pakistan Journal of Biological Sciences, 18*(1), 11-18 doi:10.3923/pjbs.2015.11.18

Fish oil:

Kiecolt-Glaser, J. K., Belury, M. A., Andridge, R., Malarkey, W. B., & Glaser, R. (2011). Omega-3 supplementation lowers inflammation and anxiety in medical students: A randomized control trial. *Brain, Behavior, and Immunity, 25*(8), 1725-1734.

Tip #69: Talk with a Licensed Therapist

Statistics:

Bureau of Labor Statistics. (2019). Occupational outlook handbook. Retrieved from bls.gov on May 22, 2020.

Tip #71: Take Control of Your Money by Managing Your Spending

Debt statistics:

Lembo Stolba, S. L. (2020, March 9). Debt reaches new highs in 2019, but credit scores stay strong. Experian. https://www.experian.com/blogs/ask-experian/research/consumer-debt-study/

College tuition data:

Kerr, E. (2019, Sept. 9). 10 most, least expensive private colleges. *U.S. News and World Report*. https://www.usnews.com/education/best-colleges/the-short-list-college/articles/10-most-least-expensive-private-colleges

Tip # 74: Cope with Social Anxiety

Data:

Anxiety and Depression Association of America. Understand the facts: Social Anxiety Disorder. Accessed May 22, 2020. https://adaa.org/understanding-anxiety/social-anxiety-disorder

Tip #83: Detach Yourself from All Screens Two Hours Before Bed

Higuchi, S., Motohashi, Y., Liu, Y., & Maeda, A. (2005). Effects of playing a computer game using a bright display on presleep physiological variables, sleep latency, slow wave sleep and REM sleep. *Journal of Sleep Research, 14*(3), 267-273.

Holzman, D. C. (2010). What's in a color? The unique human health effect of blue light. *Environmental Health Perspectives, 118*(1), A22–A27. https://doi.org/10.1289/ehp.118-a22

Benefits of blocking blue light:

Burkhart, K., & Phelps, J. R. (2009). Amber lenses to block blue light and improve sleep:

A randomized trial. *Chronobiology International, 26*(8),1602-1612.

doi:10.3109/07420520903523719

Wei, X., She, C., Chen, D., Yan, F., Zeng, J., Zeng, L., & Wang, L. (2013). Blue-light-

blocking intraocular lens implantation improves the sleep quality of cataract

patients. *Journal of Clinical Sleep Medicine, 9*(8), 741-745. doi:10.5664/jcsm.2908

Tip #90: Be Careful What You Eat and Drink Before Bed

Benefits of cherry juice:

Pigeon, W. R., Carr, M., Gorman, C., & Perlis, M. L. (2010). Effects of a tart cherry juice

beverage on the sleep of older adults with insomnia: A pilot study. *Journal of Medicinal

Food, 13*(3), 579–583. https://doi.org/10.1089/jmf.2009.0096

Effects of caffeine:

Drake, C., Roehrs, T., Shambroom, J., & Roth, T. Caffeine effects on sleep taken 0, 3, or

6 hours before going to bed. *Journal of Clinical Sleep Medicine, 9*(11), 1195-1200.

doi:10.5664/jcsm.3170.

Tip #93: Set and Maintain a Sleep Schedule

Van Dongen, H. P. A., & Dinges, D. F. (2003). Investigating the interaction between the homeostatic and circadian processes of sleep-wake regulation for the prediction of waking neurobehavioral performance. *Journal of Sleep Research, 12*(3), 181-187. https://doi.org/10.1046/j.1365-2869.2003.00357.x.

Tip #96: Try Melatonin and Other Natural Supplements

Dollins, A. B., Zhdanova, I. V., Wurtman, R. J., Lynch, H. J., & Deng, M. H. (1994). Effect of inducing nocturnal serum melatonin concentrations in daytime on sleep, mood, body temperature, and performance. *Proceedings of the National Academy of Sciences of the United States of America, 91*(5), 1824–1828. https://doi.org/10.1073/pnas.91.5.1824

Ferracioli-Oda, E., Qawasmi, A., & Bloch, M. H. (2013). Meta-analysis: Melatonin for the treatment of primary sleep disorders. *PloS One, 8*(5), e63773. https://doi.org/10.1371/journal.pone.0063773

Scheer, F. A. J. L., & Czeisler, C. A. (2005). Melatonin, sleep, and circadian rhythms. *Sleep Medicine Reviews, 9*(1), 5-9.

Tip #97: Experiment with CBD Oil

Babson, K. A., Sottile, J., & Morabito, D. (2017). Cannabis, cannabinoids, and sleep: A review of the literature. *Current Psychiatry Reports, 19,* Article 23. https://doi.org/10.1007/s11920-017-0775-9

Teitelbaum, J. (2019). A hemp oil, CBD, and marijuana primer: Powerful pain, insomnia, and anxiety-relieving tools. *Alternative Therapies in Health and Medicine,* Supplement 2, Ftune oVol. 25, 21-23.